Raven and the Rock

Storytelling in Chukotka

Raven and the Rock

Storytelling in Chukotka

Kira Van Deusen

University of Washington Press

Seattle and London

Canadian Circumpolar Institute (CCI) Press

Edmonton

Copyright © 1999 by the University of Washington Press
Printed in the United States of America
Designed by Pamela Canell Chaus

Library of Congress Cataloging-in-Publication Data
Van Deusen, Kira. 1946–
   Raven and the rock : storytelling in Chukotka / Kira Van Deusen.
    p. cm.
   Includes bibliographical references and index.
   ISBN 0-295-97841-4 (cloth : alk. paper).—ISBN 0-295-97842-2 (paper :
alk. paper)
    1. Chukchi—Folklore.   2. Yupik Eskimos—Folklore.   3. Tales—
Russia (Federation)—Chukchi Peninsula.   4. Legends—Russia (Federation)
—Chukchi Peninsula.   I. Title.
GR203.2.C5V36   1999   99–31842
398.2'0957'7—DC21   CIP

Canadian Cataloguing-in-Publication Data
Van Deusen, Kira, 1946–
   Raven and the rock
   (The Circumpolar research series, ISSN 0838-133X; no. 7)
   Includes bibliographical references and index.
   ISBN 1-896445-16-0
    1. Chukchi—Folklore.   2. Yupik Eskimos—Folklore.   3. Tales—Russia
(Federation)—Chukchi Peninsula.   4. Legends—Russia (Federation)—Chukchi
Peninsula.   I. Canadian Circumpolar Institute.   II. Title.   III. Series.
GR203.2.C5V36   1999   398.2'0957'7   C99–910728-3

The paper used in this publication is acid-free and recycled from 10 percent post-
consumer and at least 50 percent pre-consumer waste. It meets the minimum
requirements of American National Standard for Information Sciences—Permanence
of Paper for Printed Library Materials, ANSI Z39.48–1984. ♾ ♻

Once a long time ago Raven was flying around on his own business. In his claws he held an enormous rock. Finally he could hold the rock no longer. He let go, and the rock fell to earth, splitting into many pieces. The biggest chunks formed the mountains and hills, the medium-sized pieces the reindeer. From the small ones came the trees and shrubs, and from the dust came the people!

—Chukchi legend

Contents

CONTENTS

Illustrations

Preface

Raven and the Rock is a collection of folktales and legends that were told to me by Chukchi and Yupik storytellers in 1993 and 1994 in northeastern Russia. These tales represent a combination of the old and the new—they are traditional tales retold in modern settings as this ancient oral tradition develops in the post-Soviet era.

When I first went to Chukotka I was embarking on a new life-work—that of participating in the art of oral storytelling. I had begun telling tales from indigenous Siberia the year before, all learned from books. In the spring of 1993 I heard them told orally for the first time. Recording, transcribing, retelling, and finally publishing the stories has been a process of getting acquainted with a tradition different from my own and understanding the place of the stories in their own culture, how they might be explained, and how they are best left alone to do their own work. The most important links in this process are the individual tellers, who tailor the stories to individual times, places, and listeners, assuring that the tradition keeps growing. All the tellers whose stories are included in this book gave their permission and in fact seemed delighted that their stories would be heard in another country—and by people of all sorts, not only scholars. We hope that the stories will contribute to communication across national boundaries.

As I began telling stories in public, I got to know the rich world of storytelling in Canada and the United States—a world based on both tradition and contemporary life. One of the things I saw was that some tellers use tales from various world cultures to show the universality of human experience, dropping some ethnic detail. Others ground their telling in the details of the tradition from which the story springs, emphasizing what is unique in each culture. While enjoying the ways stories unite us, I quickly found myself attracted to this second approach, which led to my travels to Chukotka to learn more about the Chukchi and Yupik through human contact.

Most of these stories were told in people's homes, and some in museums and community centers. I asked simply to hear old tales and legends, usually the teller's own favorites. Sometimes I was alone with the teller and sometimes I was in the company of museum and cultural workers who had their own questions and concerns. This often had an influence on the teller's comfort—usually for the better—and possibly on some story choices.

These storytellers represent several generations of Chukchi and Yupik carriers of culture. Their tales are a cross section of an oral tradition that is very much alive, even though tales are not told in the same circumstances they were before the Soviet period. In translating the tales I have tried to retain the unique voices and styles of the tellers, as much as is possible in another language. Any small changes that take place when I tell the stories orally have been dropped in the written versions. Most of the tellers told each tale twice for my tape recordings—once in their native language and then again in Russian.

In general, members of the older generation are most comfortable with the native language, speaking it as their mother tongue. They are the last to remember the old way of life and the occasions and purposes of storytelling in the pre-Soviet period. They also share rare reminiscences about shamans of earlier times. Already as I write, many of these people are no longer living. Tellers from about forty to sixty years of age tend to be fully bilingual. This middle generation is an active group of teachers, poets, and collectors of folklore. Together with members of the younger generation, who use storytelling mostly in their work with children, these people are adapting traditional tales to modern purposes. Those under thirty-five are weaker in the native languages, and some are monolingual in Russian. The stories told by elders Lena Naukeke and Nununa were translated into Russian from Chukchi and Yupik, respectively, by relatives present at the telling. The translations from Russian to English are my own. The subtleties involved in each teller's degree of comfort in speaking Russian, as well as where tellers learned their tales and whether they tell them regularly in contemporary context, are discussed in the text.

The stories in this collection, while far from being a comprehensive introduction to the folklore of the region, represent the tales uppermost in the minds of tellers in the early post-Soviet period. They show the values tellers admire and the lessons they wish to convey to their own youths and to outsiders. Most of the themes and motifs in Chukchi and Yupik folklore show up here: the despised orphan, the girl who refuses to marry, the actions of evil spirits, and the symbolic nature of bones, hair, and the forces of the natural world.

There has never been any idea of ownership of stories in the oral traditions of Chukotka. Tales were freely exchanged at trade fairs and holiday celebrations. Even personal songs are sometimes sung by others. During my research, if tellers didn't want something retold, they simply requested confidentiality (if what they were telling sounded like gossip) or didn't tell it to me. This often included information about shamans, which is today much more freely expressed throughout Siberia than it was during my visits to Chukotka in 1993–94.

In approaching a storyteller, I always explain that I tell tales myself and would like to retell theirs orally and in writing in North America to help Americans and Canadians get acquainted with their culture. Over the last eight years this approach has without exception come as a surprise to the tellers. Indigenous people in Russia have not encountered outsiders other than folklorists and anthropologists who want to hear their tales. They also rarely encounter anyone who asks permission, because the Soviet approach assumed the rights of the collector to the material, in the name of Marxist ethnography. And so I explain about the traditions of ownership of tales in my own home area and about the North American storytelling movement, which is also an unfamiliar phenomenon to them.

The relationship of an outsider to a very different culture is a delicate one. In my discussions with indigenous people in Siberia, what has emerged is that there *is* some resentment toward those who take things away and return nothing. For years both objects and stories have made their way from Chukotka to archives in Russia, only to become inaccessible to those from whom they were taken. In some cases irreplaceable tapes have been destroyed and sacred sites disrupted. This is a familiar story in North America as well.

The other thing indigenous people resent is analysis of their culture in terms of outside structures. This is why I have attempted to keep analysis to a minimum in this book, emphasizing context instead. Although it is tempting to look at the tales in terms of Western psychology and folkloristics, I feel it is inappropriate to do so. By trying to fit another culture into our own frameworks, we can easily miss what is unique, as well as the opportunity to challenge our own assumptions. Thus I believe it is important simply to present the stories in context and allow them to speak for themselves.

In addition to keeping track of history and educating young people, storytelling fulfilled a spiritual role in traditional Chukchi and Yupik society, helping to keep human beings in harmony with nature. Although their focus is different from that of traditional healers and ceremonialists, Siberian storytellers share the shaman's gifts of inner vision, inspiration, and the ability to call spirits, cure illnesses, and predict the future. Many of the stories in this collection have shamanic content in terms of imagery and form. Tales of transformation and magic are based in the same worldview as the mystic journey of the shaman who restores lost souls and communicates with spirits of nature. Some have the form of a heroic journey. Images from the time of creation inspire creative action in present time. Shamans and storytellers maintain the contacts between the physical and spiritual worlds, and their life stories form an important part of Chukotka's history.

One more aspect of shamanic culture apparent in the storytelling tradition is that of humor and trickery. The trickster is an important figure in many magic tales, offering a humorous view of the unpredictability of life and human foibles. Laughter raises energy for shamanic ceremonies, confirming a kind of earthiness in voyages to other worlds. Humor also gives people courage to face hardships such as long winters. On several occasions the late-nineteenth-century researcher Waldemar Bogoras heard a storyteller end his tale with the words, "There! I have killed the wind!" Bogoras says that storytellers had the ability to call the spirits of animals to hunters, another ability they shared with shamans.

Traditional magic tales existed not in isolation from each other but as part of a large network that explored the variety in human character and the outcomes of behavior in the physical and spiritual worlds. (I use the Russian term "magic tale" instead of the more common English "fairy tale" because it describes the Arctic tales better and avoids negative connotations.) The tales often contain lessons about practical, environmental, and spiritual matters, and they can be tailored to meet the needs of a specific audience. Ancient tales can be told as allegories for current events. They are always multilayered vehicles for spiritual truth. Although tellers say they have learned tales precisely as told by their parents, it is understood that changes can be made and new tales and details created from the vision of the teller.

Legends, on the other hand, cannot be changed. And no matter how fantastic legendary events may seem, they are accepted as literal truth. They are true in the spiritual world if not in the physical. Today the practical teaching tale, formed from magic tale or legend by a shift in emphasis, has become more predominant than it was in the past, mainly because of the impact of the secular Soviet school system and its ideology. Teaching has come to eclipse much of the spiritual and historical function of storytelling. Stories that were explicitly spiritual or that glorified national heroes were forbidden under the Soviet system, as were shamanic ceremonies.

My first motivation in collecting Chukchi and Yupik stories was interest in the tellers and the tales themselves, as well as in cultural exchange. As storytellers opened their lives to me, I began to see how the oral tradition fit into traditional and contemporary life. Later I came to see a historical and comparative value in this collection as well. Some of the tales in this book have direct parallels with oral literature from peoples of North America, notably the raven tales.

In the late nineteenth and early twentieth centuries the Russian ethnographer W. Bogoras made an extensive folklore collection. I examined his *Chukchee Mythology* and *The Eskimo of Siberia* for correspondences with the tales I heard. His Chukchi collection includes forty-seven tales and legends; mine has twelve. He published sixteen Yupik tales; I recorded thirteen, plus fragments and anecdotes. I found in his collection several tales that I heard told, and the recurrence of many other themes or motifs. Many of these also appear in the editions of the Russian folklorists E. M. Menovshchikov and O. E. Baboshina, who collected and published tales in the middle of the twentieth century. Comparing today's tales with those collected a century ago, we find the older tales more violent, more scatological, and more sexual. A good example of this is the myth that serves as the epigraph for this book. In 1993 Raven created the earth from a rock; a hundred years earlier he created it by defecating. Although the peoples of Chukotka were little influenced by Christian moralizing, ideas brought in by the Soviet school system also served to "clean up" the stories.

In this book I use the Library of Congress system of transliteration of the Cyrillic alphabet. For ease of reading, however, certain names are transcribed in their familiar English forms, such as Alexei and Providenia instead of Aleksei and Provideniia.

Many indigenous people use Russian names. Whereas in person I used the polite Russian style of name and patronymic, in the book I often conform to English convention by using either the first or last name. Some elders, such as Nununa, use only one name, as they did in the time before Russian contact.

The picture that emerges from this journey is one of a changing and lively storytelling tradition in which old tales are told in new settings and new tales are formed from life stories. I hope this book helps to reconnect stories across the Bering Strait and to bridge the gap between practitioners of the arts and those who study them. I am grateful to all those who made my work possible by sharing their gifts of story and hospitality and teaching me some small part of their own patience, acceptance, and humor.

I would specifically like to thank the many people who helped in preparing this book. Svetlana Chuklinova, Valentina Itevtegina, Lyubov (Lyuba) Kutylina, Antonina Kymytval, Ivan Nagalyuk, Gleb Nakazik, Lena Naukeke, Nina Notai, Nununa, Alla Panaug'ye, Ekaterina Reultineut, Valentina Rintuv'ye, Galina Tagrina, Margarita Takakava, Nina Trapeznikova, and Viktor Tymnev'ye all shared stories and traditional knowledge. Workers at the Providenia Regional Museum and the Chukotka Department of Culture were of enormous help, as were Alexei Burykin, Peter Merker, and our hosts, Svetlana and Alexei Tkalich and Irina and Vladimir Podgorbunskikh. Thanks also to the Anadyr Regional Museum and the Chukotka Regional Center for Folk Culture.

On this side of the water, my heartfelt thanks to Bruce Grant, who has patiently guided me through many stages of this process. David and Andrea Spalding, Kay Stone, Julie Cruikshank, and three anonymous readers made valuable suggestions on earlier drafts of the manuscript. I am also grateful to Nikolai Vakhtin and Igor Krupnik for information, to Murray Shoolbraid and Michael Ballantyne of the British Columbia Folklore Society for compiling the index of motifs, and to the editors at the University of Washington

Press, especially Michael Duckworth, who was unfailingly encouraging and helpful. Thanks to Murray Pleasance for his photographs, which appear on pages 16, 19, 35, 36, 42, 43, 44, 58, 62, 63, 64, 65, 72, 73, and 84. (All the other photos are mine.) And to the many friends who encouraged me in this work, my deepest gratitude.

Raven and the Rock

Storytelling in Chukotka

Introduction

The region known as Chukotka, whose political status since the fall of the Soviet Union is analogous to that of a state or province of Russia, lies just below the Arctic Circle. Yet people have lived in its harsh environment for thousands of years. Some say the first people came to the northeast corner of Asia as much as twenty-seven thousand years ago. And if the ancestors of North American peoples came across the Bering land bridge, then there must have been a population in Chukotka before that bridge became impassable ten thousand years ago. Petroglyphs at Pegtymel on the coast of Chukotka date to the late Neolithic and show people hunting reindeer and whales, as well as people wearing hats resembling the "magic" mushroom *Amanita muscaria*. All of this indicates that traditional activities and even some ceremonial traditions familiar in the twentieth century were already in place at that time.

Although there are other indigenous peoples living in Chukotka today, namely the Even, Evenk,[1] Koriak, and Chuvan, most of my meetings have been with Chukchi and Yupik.[2] This book concentrates on their history and stories.

The ancestors of today's Chukchi are thought to have moved from the south, possibly from around present-day Mongolia, about two thousand years ago. Today the Chukchi number some eleven thousand to fifteen thousand. In the past, most Chukchi were tundra dwellers, keeping herds of up to ten thousand reindeer. A smaller number lived along the shore, hunting the walrus, seals, and whales of the Bering Sea.

Reindeer were basic to the tundra Chukchi way of life, providing food and transportation. Unlike some of their northern neighbors, the Chukchi

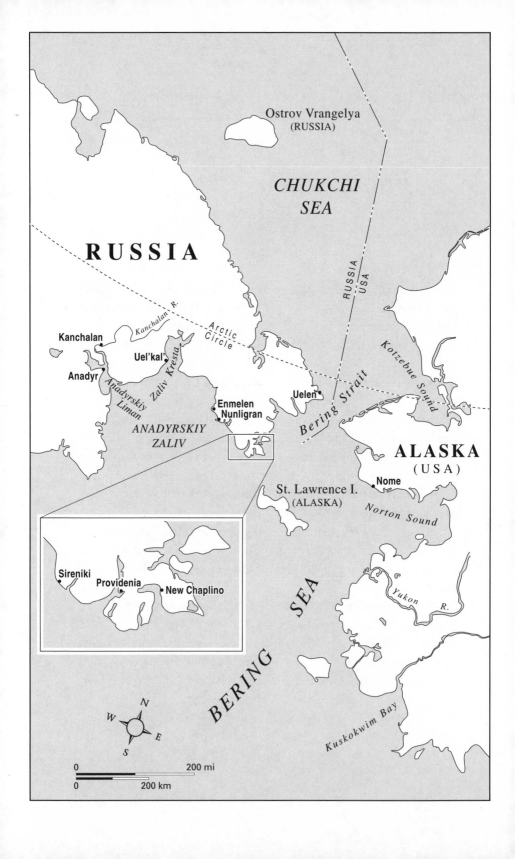

did not ride reindeer, nor did they milk them, but used them to pull sleighs and for meat. Clothing and tent covers were made from reindeer hides. And in spite of the importation of snowmobiles and Western-style clothing, many tundra dwellers still use reindeer in the same ways their ancestors did.

Seasonal rituals and ancient stories bring to mind the constant connections between human beings and the reindeer who sustain their lives. Chukchi shore dwellers depended in the same way on walrus and whales, which dominated their stories as well as sustaining their lives.

The Siberian Yupik, numbering about fifteen hundred, live mainly in a handful of villages along the shore in the Providenia region. They have been in the area much longer than the Chukchi—probably from the late Paleolithic, somewhere between four thousand and ten thousand years ago. In the last few years they have reestablished ties with their Yupik relatives in Alaska, which were broken in the late 1950s when the border was closed. They are also related by language and culture to the Inuit of Canada, the Inupiaq of Alaska, and the Kalaadlit, or Inuit, of Greenland. Their traditional way of life involved sea hunting, and their villages were settled for centuries in the most auspicious places along the coast—places that provided open access to the ocean and at the same time to lakes for freshwater and to the tundra for collecting roots and berries. Under the communist administration, many of these villages were moved, for military and other reasons, to places much less suitable.

The Chukchi and Yupik were active traders—among themselves and with neighboring indigenous peoples, and later with Russians and, after the sale of Alaska, with Americans. Shore and tundra dwellers exchanged seal oil, used for cooking and in lamps, for reindeer skins used to make clothing and tent covers. Straps made of sea mammal skin were essential to herders, just as shore dwellers needed wooden poles from the distant forests for their houses. As outsiders arrived, indigenous people traded furs for guns, beads, tea, red dye,[3] and other imported goods. The Chukchi successfully transformed the Russian taxation system (*iasak*) into an opportunity for trade by demanding gifts in return for the tribute they paid.[4] Besides trading goods, people exchanged news and stories at trade fairs.

Map of Eastern Chukotka and the Bering Strait. (Produced by Barry Levely, Cartography Unit, University of Waterloo, Ontario.)

A tundra Chukchi couple. The woman is wearing a traditional one-piece reindeer-skin *kerker*.

The Chukchi language was used for trade with other indigenous peoples. Yupik elders explain that this was because the Chukchi language is simpler than their own, and also because the Chukchi were more numerous and moved around more. As a result, they became wealthier, and their language dominated. But they always helped their shore neighbors in times of trouble.

Russians came to Chukotka in the seventeenth century. The first Cossacks and traders came from the Kolyma River area, led by the explorers Dezhnev and Alexeev in 1648, looking for sable and walrus ivory. In the next century Vitus Bering made his famous explorations of the coasts of Chukotka and Alaska. Some Cossacks married indigenous women and settled into the permanent population.

The conquest of Siberia, contrary to views commonly held in Russia even today, was neither easy nor gentle. The historian James Forsyth wrote: "In the extreme north-east, the Koriaks and Chukchi offered the most determined resistance of all [to the tsarist Russian state], facing an explicitly genocidal campaign by the Russians up to the 1750s. In the end the government decided that the war against the Chukchi should be abandoned, so that until the early twentieth century they had the unique official status of being 'not completely subdued' and were not troubled much by the Russian authorities."5 Equally unsuccessful were attempts by tsarist Russia to convert the indigenous peoples to the Orthodox church.

Most of our information on the culture and oral traditions of Chukotka in the nineteenth century comes from the works of Waldemar Bogoras. He spent ten years in Chukotka in the 1890s, exiled from central Russia for revolutionary activities as part of the movement called "People's Will." Later he and his wife, Sofia, returned with the Jesup expedition from the American Museum of Natural History in New York. Bogoras learned to speak the tundra Chukchi language fluently, wrote exhaustively about material and spiritual culture, and compiled bilingual collections of tales, while Sofia was responsible for most of the collection of ethnographic objects brought back to the museum.6 They traveled under the most rigorous of conditions, carrying large-format cameras and wax cylinder phonographs. In spite of Bogoras's cultural bias and the fact that he learned less about women's traditions than about men's, his books are a precious resource, used not only by folklorists and ethnographers but by Chukchi people themselves in reviving their rituals.

Before the restructuring of society that took place after the 1917 revolution, strong family ties ruled Chukchi and Yupik conduct. The Siberian Yupik had a strict clan structure, with the strongest clans controlling the best hunting grounds, living places, and burial grounds. Bogoras maintained that clan ties among the Chukchi were very loose, amounting only to living in the same camp. This arrangement could change year by year. Although he said that the maritime Chukchi had no clans, recent scholarship refutes his conclusion. In interviews conducted in the 1960s and 1970s by Igor Krupnik and others, maritime Chukchi people recalled clan names and complex family trees from the time of Bogoras.7

Among the Chukchi, both men and women were allowed to take a second spouse under certain circumstances, which assured that their children would be cared for in case of an unexpected death. Although this practice was outlawed under communism, the songs and dances that accompanied the marriage ceremonies are still remembered. Holidays revolved around the changing of the seasons and the lives of the reindeer and sea mammals. Prayers, sacrifices, and symbolic acts kept people in harmony with the cycle of nature.

Trade and settlement increased throughout the nineteenth century, bringing goods and ideas from the outside. Conflict frequently arose between local people and Russians who were unscrupulous and predatory in their trading activities. Protection from this exploitation was one rationale for the centralized approach to administration taken in Chukotka after the 1917 revolution.[8] Years later, the balance of power has changed little.

After the 1917 revolution, Bogoras played an important role in the Committee of the North, formed in the 1920s to deal with issues surrounding indigenous peoples. He favored the creation of American-style reservations (an idea that was not adopted) and was instrumental in sending many "missionary-ethnographers" both to study minority peoples and to convert them to the new ideology.[9]

In the early Soviet period there were two schools of thought on policy concerning minority peoples. The conservative goal was to allow indigenous peoples to sustain their culture and way of life, whereas the official majority view of the Communist party was to merge all ethnic groups in one "Soviet people."[10] Russians were seen as the "big brothers" in this merger, who would help non-Russian peoples on the path to progress.

The debate over whether to establish reserved lands for native peoples was resolved in favor of policies of assimilation. Among other things, this was seen as the road leading more easily to industrial development and exploitation of mineral resources. In 1938, minority peoples lost the special legal status they had been granted by the Committee of the North. The approach of introducing new policies locally by ethnographers was discredited under Stalin.[11]

The function of ethnography in the early Soviet period had lasting implications for anyone doing ethnographic work in the present. Experience leads local people to examine an outsider's motives and affiliations. One frequently hears about cases in which people never received back the results of research done with them. They wonder what purpose it served, suspecting that it might have been political. At first I felt that people were questioning me closely to see where I fit into the power hierarchy in both

Chukotka and my own country. My lack of institutional affiliation led at first to a certain confusion but later to greater openness and acceptance of me simply as a human being interested in stories.

Policies of collectivization adopted in the 1930s brought major changes to the Chukchi and Yupik way of life. When the *kolkhoz,* loosely translated as "collective farm," came to Chukotka, resistance was strong. Many indigenous people slaughtered whole herds of animals rather than submit to this new way of life. The Chukchi were some of the last people to be collectivized, but they, too, slaughtered up to half of their reindeer in protest.[12] This was devastating to those who had already lost many reindeer during the political and social anarchy that followed immediately upon the 1917 revolution.[13] In the 1970s and later, people were still speaking of this in hushed voices as a dangerous topic.[14]

Few understood or accepted the concept of electing representatives to local soviets (councils) formed by the new government. Their traditional sense of equality also ran counter to the new regime's effort to find exploiters (*kulaks*) among the Chukchi. In many cases wealthy herders had taken care of poor relatives and widows. Now many of these caregivers were deprived of their belongings and imprisoned.[15] And the perceived lack of clan structure created a difficulty for the communist organizers, because they were trained to organize around existing clans.[16]

Before the communist period, people had turned to shamans for ceremonials, healing, and help with difficult problems. Shamans were also some of the best storytellers, preserving history and enriching culture with their visions. Shamans, both men and women, underwent a severe period of initiation in which they became well acquainted with the geography and internal laws of the worlds of spirit. After that they were able to see clairvoyantly and to help their families and neighbors, journeying in altered states of consciousness to bring back souls stolen by evil spirits. Shamans were widely respected as community leaders and often opposed the new regime. For this they were harshly persecuted during the 1930s and later—ending their lives in the gulags. Just as the "kulaks," or wealthy reindeer herders, were considered economically backward, shamans were considered culturally backward. As people enjoying high respect in their communities, they were also targeted as exploiters. They are remembered now as healers, storytellers, leaders, and visionaries. Their wisdom about living in harmony with nature has much to offer to people dealing with today's environmental problems.

Another presence in Chukotka is that of the gulags, which left their ugly marks on the landscape and on the souls of Chukotka's inhabitants. Beginning in the 1930s the area came under the control of the Main Administration of the Northern Sea Route, the mining company Dalstroi, and the NKVD (later KGB), which together were responsible for the mines and labor camps. Tracking escaped prisoners became a dubious new occupation for those who knew the tundra, and the environment was damaged by the mines. Chukchi and Even people were required to provide food and transportation for Dalstroi.

In spite of serious resistance, collectivization was considered complete by the 1950s, bringing with it enforced settlement of nomadic people, residential school education, and moving of villages. Valuable resources, from reindeer meat and sable skins to gold, coal, and natural gas, were taken out of Chukotka to feed the national economy.

Some relatively worthless material goods came back to Chukotka; they were considered an insult compared with what had been taken. This insult is still remembered and resented. When discussing what would make good gifts for storytellers, my contacts advised me to bring things that would be truly useful, and certainly not frivolous items such as cosmetics that would only remind people of past injuries.

After the death of Stalin in 1953 there was a large influx of immigrant workers. Because people who came to Chukotka from other areas of the USSR received wage bonuses and other benefits, this differential in earnings also contributed to friction between local people and "incomers."[17] Native people were no longer needed as workers, and some of their settlements were closed.

The organizational basis of herding changed, too. Instead of moving in family groups, herders were now professionals—and mostly men. This meant that they had to live apart from their families, and some never married at all. The facilities provided for the women and children in villages failed to live up to the ideal, with cold, poorly constructed houses and boarding schools that served mostly canned goods instead of healthy traditional food. An increase in modern medical facilities was offset by the unhealthy change in diet.

In the early Soviet years, educational policies led to the creation of writing systems based on the Latin alphabet for previously unwritten languages, including Chukchi and Yupik. Native languages were used in schools, but in a form that was standardized in terms of both regional and gender variations. Later, new alphabets were created based on Cyrillic. As boarding schools that accompanied collectivization replaced village schools, the Russian language was enforced and native languages forbidden.[18] This policy of assimilation was not actually published but was everywhere understood and implemented.[19] In spite of these policies and the fact that Russian teachers were sometimes guilty of alcoholism, embezzling, and sexual abuse,[20] literacy rose sharply.[21] This learning against strong odds might have been a result of the native people's strong interest in literature, based on their own oral traditions.

With children away in boarding schools, contact between generations weakened, and much traditional knowledge was lost. Oral traditions, along with shamanism, suffered both from the process of social change and from explicit policies against them, as well as from the loss of the strongest carriers of culture.

In the 1950s and 1960s, a new form of labor organization was introduced, parallel to the *kolkhoz* and in many cases replacing it. The *sovkhoz,* or state farm, was an enormous amalgamation that replaced the cooperative with a wage economy and increased the export of resources. Private hunting and fishing were forbidden. On the plus side, incorporation into the Soviet Union brought higher education, contact with the rest of the country, and electricity.

Many Chukchi and Yupik still work with reindeer and hunt sea mammals, while others practice contemporary professions, especially in medicine and education. They live in cities and towns, not only in Chukotka but all over Russia, although northern people often tend to return home. Since the collapse of the Soviet Union the economic situation has worsened, but privatization of herding may bring back some aspects of an earlier way of life, replacing the reindeer "brigade" (composed of unrelated workers) with old-style family units. In the early 1990s Chukotka was separated from Magadan Oblast (Province). People had high hopes that their economic situation would improve with greater autonomy and local control, but in fact it has not. As goods and services from the center dry up, people work toward self-reliance.

Today Chukotka, like the rest of Russia, is fraught with economic, social, and ecological problems. Nine time zones and seven thousand kilometers from Moscow, Chukotka is at the far end of a communication and transportation network that has almost completely broken down since *perestroika*. By 1993–94, more goods had started to come from Alaska than from central Russia, but they were very expensive and got no farther than the regional centers. In distant villages, people receive no pay for months on end. Everywhere there is little to eat. Vodka is available when not much else is, having become a medium of exchange as well as a medium of forgetfulness. Vodka causes many deaths, through accidents and fights and by exacerbating health problems. The rate of tuberculosis in Chukotka is almost five times that of the nation as a whole.[22] People die young. Recent reports show that "the average life expectancy of members of the Northern Minorities is between 40 and 45 years, about 16–18 years less than the average in the Russian Federation." The suicide rate is 80–90 per 100,000.[23] Wage differentials between Russian incomers and native people (when wages are received at all) can be three times or more.[24] Although "incomers" who have lived in Chukotka for many years show greater appreciation and respect for indigenous people than do those who have come more recently, racism is still a major issue. The most popular form of ethnic joke throughout Russia is the "Chukchi joke," although oddly enough it is not always the Chukchi who appears foolish in it.

In certain parts of the tundra, people continue to live in the ancient, traditional way, but even the animals are less healthy and plentiful than they were in the past. Reindeer have been affected by mining and by the dumping of nuclear waste in the Arctic Ocean. People are less familiar with medicinal and food plants than their ancestors were, and young men do not undergo the rigorous physical training that was the traditional preparation for herding. In the spring, herdsmen are literally on their feet running all day. Great endurance, quick reflexes, and precise understanding of nature are needed, and young people are poorly prepared for this way of life.

International law has had some effects on the lives of sea hunters. When Chukotka first became open to foreign tourism, local people hoped to be able to sell souvenirs made of walrus ivory and sealskin, but these activities have been circumscribed by the U.S. Marine Mammal Protection Act, which bans any import of these items to the United States. Another limitation came from the International Whaling Commission's policy with regard to bowhead whaling. The Soviet Union had stopped hunting bowhead whales in the early 1970s (prior to that it was done not by individual families but by special whaling boats). The people of Chukotka received official permission from the IWC to hunt bowhead whales again only in the fall of 1997.[25] Walrus hunting in Chukotka is also limited by the United States–Russia walrus agreement, but native harvests on both sides of the international boundary have never approached the critical level set by the agreement.[26]

Chukotka's rich environment has been severely damaged. Whalers in Sireniki village say they have taken only two whales in twenty years; walrus and seals are also much less plentiful than they once were. Even if young people had the necessary skills, it is questionable whether the environment could sustain today's population.

Ekaterina Reultineut, former director of the Chukchi national dance ensemble, Ergyron, expressed to me the deep concern felt by many for the environment. "This is a rich place, but we need to use it carefully. There are problems with overfishing—the fish are not going up the rivers any more. The search for gold in the rivers leading to the Arctic Ocean destroys a lot of whitefish and, around Anadyr, salmon. And the land—if even the top five centimeters is disturbed it will not recover. That is enough to destroy the plants. People are not careful in taking gas out. I also worry about those people who are coming to steal the golden root [a medicinal plant related to ginseng, Sedum roseum], the bear's gallbladder, and the reindeer antlers.

"Ancestral graves have been desecrated by building military sites on the places where people used to live. Further desecration has come more recently as fortune hunters learn the value of archaeological objects."

Today local and federal associations of indigenous people are working for political redress and control of the land while others work on environmental, economic, and cultural issues. Healing the environment and healing the spirit go hand in hand. Essential to this healing is listening to the wisdom of the elders, the stories handed down from generation to generation. Most of the shamans have disappeared, but people still turn to their elders to learn about the past. Traditional knowledge contains not only the spiritual basis of civilization, the history of a people's inner and outer life, but also valuable lessons about living wisely on the earth.

1 / Anadyr

A female walrus was out in the water looking at the shore during one of the big holidays. She saw people in beautiful clothes walking along the shore.

"I'd like to make myself some clothes like that," she thought. She came up on land and made herself lovely things to wear. Then she went walking flirtatiously along the shore.

A hunter came out and saw her. "Who is that beautiful woman?" he thought. "I'd like to marry her!"

He approached her.

The walrus-woman looked around and saw him. "Oh no, a hunter!" she said. "He's going to shoot me and eat me." And she rushed away back into the sea!

—Valentina Itevtegina

Although Chukotka is very close to North America, separated from Alaska only by the narrow Bering Strait, it was not an easy place to get to in 1993. Special invitations were necessary to get visas, and transportation was difficult. My husband, Murray, and I flew to Chukotka from the coastal city of Magadan on April 17, 1993, at the invitation of performing artists Svetlana and Alexei Tkalich, whom we had met the previous summer in Whitehorse.

We boarded our Aeroflot plane the requisite several hours late and received a cheery greeting from the copilot, who spoke English. Flying north, we saw mountains and hills and the networks of rivers snaking their way across the tundra to the sea. They formed patterns that reminded me of embroidery or carvings, traceries that repeat themselves in the veins of leaves and the markings on animals. Although we were too high to see ravens or reindeer, we got an idea of the lay of the land: open tundra, rugged shoreline, muted grays and greens, no trees.

After we were in the air the copilot invited us up to the cockpit, where we drank tea and watched nervously as his eight-year-old son played with knobs and switches. We tried to assure ourselves that the father would not allow this game if there were anything unsafe about it. But a couple of years later I thought of this moment again on reading news reports of a Russian plane that had crashed, killing all aboard—with a child at the controls.

Two hours later we landed in Anadyr. As the plane touched the ground it immediately went into a skid and slithered to a stop on the runway. Welcome to Chukotka!

Svetlana was there to meet us, in spite of the time lag. Late planes are to be expected in Chukotka. Delays of a week are not unusual, due mostly to the weather but increasingly to problems with undermaintained planes and lack of fuel. Svetlana was good-natured about our lateness.

We had met Svetlana and her husband, Alexei, the previous summer at the Yukon International Storytelling Festival, where I was their interpreter. Although Russians themselves, they stunned audiences with Chukchi stories, songs, and dances. They came from Anadyr, the regional capital, a city of about twelve thousand, the largest by far in Chukotka.

Over Christmas dinner at our place on Hornby Island, British Columbia, we four thought about producing a photograph album about Chukotka and its storytelling and arts and crafts. We were the perfect group—Alexei knew traditional culture, Svetlana specialized in beadwork, sewing, and other traditional crafts, Murray was a professional photographer, and I could write the text. It seemed like a marvelous plan, and sure enough, a few months later we were landing in Chukotka, ready to dive in.

It turned out we had a lot to learn about post-*perestroika* Russia, about the north and its peculiarities of time, weather, and transport, about relations between Russians and indigenous people, about research, and about ourselves. But that, of course, came later. For now we were ready to go!

My first impression of Chukotka was of its bareness—not a tree anywhere to be seen. Tiny tundra mosses were just beginning to appear from under the snow at the end of April. This was a stark contrast to the western Canadian rain forest where I live, lush with huge trees and green plants. The

The city of Anadyr. The coal burner in the center of town provides heat and hot water to all the buildings. Hot water runs over the ground in pipes like that shown in the foreground.

city of Anadyr was made up of unimaginative big concrete buildings set up on stilts to avoid melting the permafrost. They were all connected by a system of poorly insulated hot-water pipes running over the ground from a central coal-burning plant that provided electricity, heat, and hot water to the whole city. At the same time it belched smoke and deposited a layer of coal dust over everything. In winter the wind blows so hard that sometimes it is impossible even to walk along the street.

Alexei was in church when we arrived—it was Russian Easter. He had become involved in the revival of Russian Orthodoxy. For the time being, church services were held in the House of Culture, a Soviet-era community center. Alexei's commitment was to become deeper and would take him further from his interests in shamans and the older ways of life of the Chukchi people he worked with in the theater. He still held a position with the

Department of Culture but was soon to exchange it for a teaching position at the pedagogical institute.

While the couple had been away in Canada, Svetlana had lost her job, but she was now working out a series of free-lance teaching appointments that would soon become an official job with the Department of Culture. Having studied the arts of beadwork, embroidery, and skin preparation with native masters, she now began going into communities to teach another generation how to teach these same skills to others.

Because Svetlana and Alexei's living accommodation was very small, we took a room at the local hotel, where we exchanged our key daily with the woman at the desk, who smiled at last on the day we left. On Saturday nights the bar got raucous, and on one early Sunday morning I found blood on the floor of the foyer.

Svetlana and Alexei said we would meet the artists and storytellers of Anadyr and then visit various villages. Time passed, and it turned out no plans had been made for these excursions. Fog was heavy, transportation expensive or nonexistent, bureaucracy difficult. We spent most of our time in Anadyr. While our stomachs adjusted to an unfamiliar diet heavy with meat and fat, Murray photographed the coal-burning electric plant, apartment buildings, and the statue of Lenin.

The insides of Anadyr's houses turned out to be as warm and welcoming as the outsides were unattractive. Northern hospitality reigns here, as it does throughout the circumpolar region. Soon my tapes filled with stories as my stomach filled with reindeer meat, pancakes, and tea. The Russian language, which I had learned in college many years before, began to flow again on my tongue and in my dreams. I heard many stories and learned a great deal about traditional culture.

And about research. For one thing, in the north you must never put off until tomorrow anything that can be done today. Tomorrow the possibility will mysteriously have disappeared. I was glad Alexei had an excellent collection of books.

My experience of Chukotka is probably typical of the place itself. There is a jerky quality to time there—for ages nothing happens and then suddenly you must rush madly. Plans change at a moment's notice. Coming from a place where for the most part things work and appointments are made and kept, it took me some time to adjust to this unpredictability. Looking back, I see my own impatience and awkwardness, but many people helped me to overcome them. In Chukotka there is no entertainment but friendship. Programs are made to be broken. People are expert at making conversation—the way to pass time and to know others. The most unlikely person may make the most fascinating companion.

There were plenty of frustrations to our month in Anadyr—and joys as well. The joys invariably involved meetings with friendly, generous people and getting to know how their lives worked. At the end of our time, we had barely made a start on a photo album, and it was not at all certain what form our book might take. We agreed to come back in the fall, when conditions would be more propitious. As it turned out, it was a whole year later that I returned alone for the second half of my research.

The first storyteller I met in 1993 was Valentina Kagievna Itevtegina. As time went by we became friends, finding unexpected things in common— an interest in music and even a particular kind of sense of humor.

Svetlana and I had walked through the snow, slipping on the icy streets, to the Anadyr Regional Museum, where we had looked at its marvelous collection of engravings on walrus tusks. Most of the engraving is done by the women of Uelen village, who have raised it to a fine art. Often stories are portrayed on the tusks, moving cartoon-fashion from one end to the other. I was thrilled to see one of the stories I tell at home portrayed there in the collection.[1]

Then we went into a sunny room at the end of the hall. A woman of about sixty with round cheeks and bright eyes was working at a desk. She looked up, full of curiosity. We were introduced rather formally, and Valentina showed us how she embroidered using the chin hair of a reindeer. The white hairs on brown reindeer suede made bright geometric patterns. She was making an eyeglasses case, which I now use daily.

Conversation lagged; the room was hot and stuffy. But we arranged that Valentina would come to our hotel soon and record a couple of stories. She came the next afternoon, and it was then that we began to relax together, get acquainted, and plan future social events.

Valentina Kagievna grew up in the 1920s in a *yaranga* (skin tent) in the village of Uelen on the north coast. She was given a childhood name that meant

Chukchi writer and storyteller Valentina Itevtegina telling the story "Wood Chips" at her grandson's birthday party.

"Woman who walks only forward," which she still thinks is appropriate. She explains that traditional Chukchi childhood names were given soon after birth. Only later did a person receive a permanent name. Evil spirits could sense a child's location from the sound of a true name, and this would be dangerous while the child was still too young to survive their attack.

Valentina explains that her family is of the walrus clan.[2] Her holiday parka has white marks on the front representing walrus tusks, wolf fur around the hood as the walrus's moustache, and wolverine fur around the hands and bottom as flippers.

Her father was a hunter, not only of walrus but of polar fox and white bear. His children and grandchildren have all distinguished themselves in professions. Valentina tells with pride of her brother, who was the first Chukchi flier, and of her daughters, one a judge and the other an expert seamstress. One son is a flier like his uncle; the other trained as a teacher and is now with the Hare Krishna people in Vladivostok—a mystery to Valentina.[3] All her children were born in a *yaranga* in Uelen, which they consider the most beautiful place on earth.

Valentina herself worked for many years as a hat maker. She can make any kind of hat, she says—hats for reindeer herders, sea hunters, fashionable ladies, and ordinary people. Although herders are often seen bareheaded, in cold Arctic weather a good hat is of the utmost importance. Now she is retired and works in the museum doing her own original embroidery and beadwork. She is an expert storyteller and has had a book of her original stories published in Chukchi, soon to be translated into Russian. She also sings her own songs. Growing up she learned the songs of her mother, her grandmother, and others. She later composed new ones using traditional themes and story motifs in modern forms—songs, poetry, and short stories.

She began by telling me stories of her own family. Valentina is proud of her father's courage and expertise on the ice. His story reminds me of tales I have read of people getting stranded on icebergs torn away from the shore. In folktales a giant rescues the hunter, and in more contemporary tales the hunter turns up at a village far from his own. Valentina's story brings mythic time into the present and reminds me how close today's city dwellers are to a traditional hunting life.

"Once when I was young, I fell down a cliff and was unconscious for a month and a half. My mother came to the hospital when I was just beginning to regain consciousness and asked what I would like to eat. I said walrus bouillon and some fresh walrus meat. This was early spring when there was nothing fresh, only meat that had been stored all winter. The ice was slushy and breaking up—nobody could go out on it, although there were walrus to be seen. But I was the only daughter among seven brothers, and my life was in danger.

"My father took his gun, a bag, and a big knife and went out, jumping from one iceberg to another. And at last he shot a walrus. He cut off a piece of meat and bits of the heart and liver, as much as would fit in his pack. And then he jumped from iceberg to iceberg, back to shore.

"People were watching in amazement. Others were trying to go out, attached by straps to someone on shore in case they fell in. And they were falling in! But my father, an old man, went out with no strap to get meat for his only daughter. Then he took the bag home.

"Mama cooked and brought meat and bouillon to the hospital. She woke me up and gave me a drink of bouillon. I drank and felt the warmth going through my arms and head, all through my body. I opened my eyes and there was Mama with tears rolling down her cheeks. 'Why are you crying?' I said. 'I'm not crying—it's hot!' she said. 'I drank some of that bouillon too!' And in fact both of us were sweating. I ate the meat and from that time my recovery began."

The traditional story Valentina tells of Raven and Fox, which follows, conveys much about the values of good hunters like her father. When Raven goes hunting, he does everything carefully. He puts on his snowshoes and walks in a way that prepares his path for return. When he hears a strange noise, his curiosity overcomes his fear and revulsion at the strange baby he pulls from the ice. He is rewarded with a good supply of fish from inside the baby's clothes, but he is careful not to take more than he needs and to lace the baby back up and put it back in the water.

Fox, on the other hand, doesn't think for herself—she just follows in Raven's footsteps. She is terrified and revolted by the strange baby, flings the fishing gear away, and runs home with nothing. "You're spoiling the best places," says Raven in reproach. He knows that the baby is a spirit. Like the forces of nature, it can be both helpful and terrifying, and like the animals people hunt, it gives food if treated well. He realizes that because Fox has offended the spirit (and lost Raven's gear), it will disappear and take the fish with it.

The second phase of the story teaches a similar lesson, but in the tundra instead of the sea. Raven carefully selects the smallest of the reindeer, and because he is not greedy, the owner of the reindeer doesn't begrudge it. Not only that, but he is able to carry the meat home to his family. The woman who owns the reindeer is probably a deity—the mother of the reindeer or of all the animals, who is known to many Siberian peoples as the provider of good hunting. Like the spirit-baby, she must be treated with affection and respect.

Fox picks the biggest reindeer, arousing first the suspicion and then the anger of the owner of the animals. Then the reindeer proves too big to carry, and Fox is presumptuous enough to expect the person she has just robbed to help her! The result of this foolish behavior is that the woman takes all the reindeer away. Certainly any hunter foolish enough to shoot the biggest reindeer will destroy the integrity of the herd, causing loss not only to himself but to all his neighbors. The hunter who takes only what he needs can always come back another day. Fox has offended the spirits of the sea and the tundra, and things will go badly not only for her but for everyone.

An interesting point that comes up in this and other stories is the power of spit. In this case it kills, but in many other cases saliva is used to heal wounds. Clearly it carries a lot of life force.

Although Raven is the hero in this story, teaching people how to hunt, he also retains some of his character as trickster in not sharing much food with Fox.[4] In many world cultures Fox is known as a trickster in her own right, who tricks Bear and other animals and sometimes helps people.[5] In this story she tries to compete with Raven, a more powerful trickster than herself, and comes out the loser.

Part of the importance of the trickster lies in humor, which plays an important role in teaching and in spiritual development. Chukchi storytellers like Valentina are well aware that lessons learned laughing stick longer than those delivered didactically. Laughter raises courage and the energy needed to solve problems such as finding enough food to survive the winter. Besides the antics of Raven and Fox, there is a shamanic joke in this story. In the usual course of things, a shaman leaves a dwelling through its smokehole to travel to other worlds. But in this story Raven and Fox look down through the smokehole into the world of spirit. Although looking down through a smokehole is more feasible in the subterranean houses typical of shore dwellers than it is in a *yaranga*, it is reminiscent of the way shamans and folktale heroes go down through the hearth to the lower world. Raven reports on what he sees the same way a shaman reports on a journey.[6] In some folktales visitors to the upper world look down on their own homes through holes in the sky.

Valentina told the tale first in Chukchi—accompanied by animated gestures that had us laughing as we tried to guess what the story was about—and then in Russian. She tells it with equal ease in both languages because she learned it from her parents in Chukchi and told it to her own children and grandchildren in both Chukchi and Russian. It is one of her favorites, partly because Raven reminds her of her father, in his devotion to his children. I was interested in the fact that Valentina includes Raven's wife in her tale, whereas she is missing in other versions. Raven's family appears much more often in tales from the Koriak and Itelmen people of Kamchatka than it does among the Chukchi. But I often notice that women include more female characters in their stories than men do, emphasizing the importance of their advice. They also have the women speak, whereas male tellers leave them silent.[7]

Raven and Fox

Long, long ago, when the animals could still talk, Raven and Fox lived next door to each other. One day Raven got up early. He went outside and thought, "Where should I go today, to the tundra or to the sea?"

He decided to go to the sea. "Maybe I'll find something that's been thrown up on shore for my children," he thought. He took his sealskin bag upon his shoulder. Raven did not fly but put on his snowshoes—raven paws, they are called. He walked on foot. It was very slippery. He walked and fell, but still he tried to make a way to come back by.

Suddenly he saw a fresh hole in the ice, with steam coming out. He looked around; it was still dark. "Who has been fishing so early? Who left me this hole?"

He took down his bag, took out his fishing gear, and threw the line in the hole. He let the line down deep and fished.

Aha! Something on the line. It's heavy.

"Must be a big fish," he thought and started to pull it out. As it got closer he heard the cry of a child, "Nga, nga!"

Raven looked. "Who has left a child here? What kind of bad mother would do a thing like that?"

As it got closer he saw it. It was scary—sparks were coming from the baby! It was crying. Closer and closer, the water got red! And then he saw a monster baby—it was terrible, with sparks coming from the mouth. It had one big eye, sharp teeth, and a big mouth.

Raven wanted to throw it back, but his curiosity got the better of him. "I'll just look it over. People don't have children like this. I've never seen anything like it." He pulled it out and put it on the ice. It was wearing baby clothes.

He opened up the front of the clothing and out came many, many fish!

He filled his bag, tied the baby back up, and put it back in the water. He put his bag on his shoulder and went home.

When he got there he woke his wife. The fox neighbor was with her babies.

"Get up quick, Mitingeut," said Raven to his wife. "While the neighbor is sleeping, get up and clean these fish."

"Oh, I feel like sleeping some more. I don't want to get up."

"Later, later. You'll go back to sleep. Hurry."

"All right," she said at last, and got up. She cooked up the fish, and a nice smell filled up the earth hut.

The neighbor woke up. "Oh, who is cooking? Where is that tasty smell coming from?"

"Never mind, wait. We will bring you something."

"I know, you'll bring me a lot of fish."

But Miti brought them just one and a half little fish.

"I told you, you should bring me lots of fish," said Fox. "This is not enough for all my little children." She cooked the little fish, woke the children, and gave them each a bit of fish and a little bit of bouillon. The day went by, and when night came everybody went to sleep.

Next day Fox woke up early. "Now where did Raven go yesterday? I want to go to the same place."

She went out. "Where will I go? To the sea or to the tundra? I'll go to the sea. I'll follow the raven's tracks. Maybe there's something still there."

She put on the raven's feet and took the raven's bag and went. She walked and walked. The ground was slippery—she fell and got up again. At last she arrived at the hole.

"Oho! Where did this fresh hole come from? Fresh steam is coming out. I'll bet Raven was fishing here yesterday. He caught lots. Now I'll catch fish too! Lots and lots, so there'll be enough for the whole winter."

Suddenly there was something on the line, something heavy. "Oh, I'll bet I have something heavy, a big one."

She pulled and pulled and heard, "Nga, nga!"

"Oh, what a fish I have here. Look at those sparks!" She pulled it out and saw the horrible big mouth and sharp teeth. The baby was crying, "Nga, nga."

Fox lost her nerve. She threw all the fishing gear into the hole, grabbed the raven's feet and bag, and ran home. She ran without looking back.

Raven was waiting outside. "Hey, where have you been?"

"Don't yell at me, I've been down by the sea. I caught a monster baby. It was terrible! Don't go there anymore, Raven. It was awful!"

"You're spoiling the good places. Where am I going to fish now?" said Raven.

The day went by. Next day Raven woke up early.

"Fox lost my fishing gear. Where am I going to get food now? I don't know. Shall I go to the sea? But I have nothing to fish with. Better go to the tundra. Maybe somebody left something behind. I'll cut off a piece of meat and bring it back."

He walked and walked and saw a huge yaranga. "So big! Who could live in such a big yaranga? I'll go look. Maybe somebody will take pity on me and give me a little piece of meat. I'll feed my children and my wife. We'll all be full."

The yaranga was very big, but he saw no door. Raven went all the way around and there was no door. "How can people get in and out? How do they live?"

He went up on the roof, and there he saw an opening. He looked in.

"Aha. A fire, smoke. This means somebody lives here. There's a pot with meat cooking in it. And what a fine smell! I'd love to eat a little piece. What else? Aha, here comes a woman. I see her. What long braids she has, she must be beautiful. She must be kind. She is looking all around. I see a big herd of reindeer, moving in the direction of the sun, moving, moving. All kinds of reindeer, spotted ones, white, brown ones. All of them are fat, big. This woman lives alone and such a herd she has! I'd like to have just one of those reindeer. Aha, there's a baby, a weak one. How will I kill that one? I'll spit at it!"

Raven spit and the reindeer fell. "What strong spit I have!"

The woman saw that the reindeer had fallen. She braided her hair. She said, "What will I do with you? You were a weak one. You're not even big enough for me to eat."

She took it by the feet and threw the baby reindeer up out of the yaranga through the smokehole. Raven quickly put it in his bag and rushed home.

"Miti, Miti, get up quick! Cook up this fresh food for the children while the neighbor is sleeping!"

Miti said, "Oh, how I want to sleep. You are waking me from such a sweet dream."

"Get up. You'll sleep more later."

She got up and slowly started to cook over the seal-oil lamp. Again such a good smell started coming.

The neighbor woke up. "Where is that delicious smell coming from?"

"Just wait, we'll bring you some."

"I know, you'll bring me a lot."

Miti took over just a rib and a half.

"I thought you were going to bring a lot. Oh well . . ." said Fox, and she put her pot over the lamp and started to cook the meat. She woke the babies and said, "Wake up, eat this." They all ate and drank the bouillon. The day went by and then they went to sleep.

Fox woke up early the next day. "Today I'll follow Raven's tracks to the tundra," she said. "Maybe I'll find a big reindeer."

She followed the tracks and saw the yaranga. "Oh, what a big yaranga. Nobody is around."

She went all the way around and saw there was no door. "How will I get up? Ah, there's a rope hanging down." She took the rope and climbed up.

She looked down through the opening. "What a good smell of meat cooking! Something cooking, good fat reindeer. So tasty! Who lives here? Oh, just one woman alone, with all these reindeer. What a beauty she is, braiding her hair. What a big herd! Which one will I choose? There's the biggest, fattest one. How will I kill it? I'll spit!"

She spit and the reindeer fell. The woman looked over. "What is happening? My reindeer are falling. Somebody is killing them. Something is wrong here. Well, if somebody wants to take reindeer dishonestly from me, let them." And with great difficulty she lifted the reindeer and pushed it out of the opening.

Fox rushed up and took out her knife. "So much meat, this will keep me for the whole winter!"

She started cutting it up and putting pieces in her sealskin bag. Then she tried to lift it. It was so heavy she could not pick it up.

"I'll try calling that woman. Maybe she is kind and will help me. Hey, woman, help me to lift this bag. Good, tasty meat, so heavy! My children are waiting for me."

"So that's who is killing my reindeer. That is the one who is making my herd small," thought the woman. "Just wait," she called, "I'll be right out. Close your eyes and wait. Put the strap from the bag over your eyes."

Fox waited.

The woman came out and took up the stick they use for treating skins. "Oh, clever fox, now you are going to get it!" She hit Fox over the head, and the fox passed out. The woman gathered everything up—the yaranga and all the reindeer—and moved away to a different place.

At last Fox woke up. "What a headache I've got. What happened? And where is that woman? She said close your eyes and I'll help you." Fox opened her eyes and looked around. What a bump she had on her head! And there was no herd, no yaranga, no food, no woman, nobody!

And that's all![8]

"That's all!" is a typical story ending. Although it may sound abrupt in translation, these words—*tauwa, fai,* or *tfai* in Yupik and the Chukchi *etset'* (female pronunciation) or *et'rech* (male pronunciation)—are an important formula. They signal that it is time for a response from the listeners, for their appreciation and questions, which are an integral part of the story. The message has been delivered.

One night Valentina invited Murray and me to dinner with her family and friends: a poet, a doctor, and the former head of the local administration. Russians refer to these people as the "Chukchi intelligentsia." Svetlana and Alexei were conspicuously not invited. They said they didn't mind, and that Valentina and her friends would talk more openly without them. They described an experience in the Yukon in which they had felt that because they were foreigners, First Nations people accepted them more openly than they would non-native Canadians.

We came into the living room, where the table was set. Against the wall opposite my seat was a huge cabinet typical of Russian apartments, full of cut glass, books, and amulets made of walrus ivory. Behind me hung a Central Asian rug. Valentina's daughter served us salads, sausages, roast chicken, fried fish, fresh cake, and *stroganina*—a popular dish made of shredded frozen fish. They call it "Chukchi ice cream." When I was so stuffed that I was sure I would never move again, Valentina said, "Now we will tell stories. You go first!"

Apparently this was a contemporary version of an old tradition in which guests are asked for stories. It was a struggle, but I managed to tell one short story—about why the Tuvan camel has no horns and only a short tail. "Your turn!" I said in conclusion.

This is the story Valentina told. It comes from Uelen, which is very close to North America. It came to mind that night because we were from the other side of the water. She told it briefly and crisply, with a certain amount of mockery about the relations between husband and wife. A couple of weeks later we were invited to another party at Valentina's, in honor of her grandson's ninth birthday. On that occasion she told the same story to the boy and his friends. That version included more detail about the way the people used to live, because these children were growing up in the city and had no experience of the traditional way of life. Here I reproduce the longer version. Both times Valentina told the story only in Russian, with a lot of laughter.

Wood Chips

I was born in the town of Uelen, located on the cape.

Long, long ago, there very few people living on the Uelen cape, just an old man and an old woman. They had no children. When they were younger, they didn't notice being lonely. They were busy—the man with hunting and the woman with sewing the yaranga and clothes. All their lives each did their own work. She looked after the yaranga as if it were a child. She washed, sewed, cooked, and fed the old man. In the summer she gathered plants in preparation for the winter. And he made straps and sleds, also getting ready for winter in his own way. He did his hunting and now he was working on his sleigh.

In Uelen the wind gets up. If the north wind blows, a big storm is coming. The sea throws all kinds of things onto the shore. And if you leave anything on the shore, the wind carries it away. When the weather gets bad in Uelen nobody comes visiting from other villages.

The people began to get bored. The old woman said, "Oh, if only somebody would come visiting. How I would love to talk to somebody. Fall is coming, and then winter. Nobody will come and we'll be so bored."

"Yes," said the old man, "We'll get bored." And he went back out to work on his sleigh. He worked with an ax, and a pile of wood chips formed beside him. Once in a while the woman would come down and take the wood chips back to start the fire. Sometimes the weather gets bad, rainy, and the chips get wet, so she liked to keep them inside.

Well, one day the wind got very strong. Again nobody would be coming. And there were many, many chips on the shore. Suddenly the old man thought, "What if I were to throw these chips out over the sea and the wind carried them across to the other side? I'll bet somebody lives over there. There must be a shore, and land. I'll throw them!"

And the wind got stronger and stronger. He threw all the wood chips. He threw them and said, "Go over to the other side. Turn into people! So there will be people over there." And the wind carried them and carried them. None were left on his shore. "Go, go to the other side. Build yourself yarangas and earth houses. Live there. And come visit us every year! You'll be our guests."

He went home happy, but he didn't tell the woman anything about it. The summer passed, and the fall. The long harsh winter came with its high winds. Then bright warm sun, and everything thawed. Then summer came again. Long white nights. And then at last it began to get darker again. And the old man was sitting on the shore, working, getting ready for winter again.

And then he got up and looked out to sea. He could see something in the distance. He looked and looked. It seemed somebody was coming. He went inside and said, "Old woman, my old woman, come and look. It looks as if somebody is coming."

She said, "Who would be coming? You're probably looking at your own eyelashes!"

He went back out. They were coming closer and closer. Maybe it was walrus? He went back to work.

Then he looked up again. They were coming closer. He rushed inside again.

"Come out! Look, guests are coming."

"What guests?"

"Come and look!"

"All right. If you're fooling me there'll be more work tomorrow."

"Come look. If there's nothing, you can come right back and get back to work."

"All right."

She came out and looked. Boats were coming closer and closer.

"Who are they, where are they coming from? Did they come from around the cape?"

"No, they came from straight across the water."

"What kind of people can they be?"

"I told you somebody was coming. Let's go greet them."

They went out on the shore. The boats came up and people got out. The old people listened to them curiously. What's that? They were speaking differently. Some different language.

The old man said, "Can you understand what they're talking about?"

"No, I don't understand a word," she said. "Who can it be?"

But the strangers brought gifts from their boats. They surrounded the old people with presents. The old man and woman looked at each other and didn't understand a word.

Those people ran here and there, carrying things, bringing presents.

The old man said, "Guests have come. Why are we sitting here? We should invite them in. They're probably hungry."

"Yes, guests," said the woman, and she ran back to the yaranga and cooked up the best foods they had. Fresh reindeer, tasty bouillon.

The old man invited the people in. They came to the yaranga and sat by the fire, and the woman fed them all. She put out the wooden dishes and cut the meat. They all ate and talked and laughed happily. The old people understood nothing the strangers were saying.

But the old woman took care of everybody. She pulled out the best skins so they could lie down. Everybody lay down on soft skins. They stayed one night, they stayed two.

Then good weather came. It was calm and clear. The oldest of them spoke in his own incomprehensible language. "Good weather," he said.

The old man realized that they were going to leave. And he understood that they said, "You have taken good care of us. You are our relatives, our parents."

"They say they are our relatives, our children. Where can these children have come from?" The old man did not understand.

30

The guests gathered everything together down on the shore, got into their boats, and sailed away.

As they were leaving, they said to the old man, "Don't you remember how you sent us over onto the other shore? So there would be life there, people there. We have back come to you. We'll come every year and bring you food and clothes. Because you are our relatives."

The old man thought, "Where can these relatives have come from? We've never been over there, or heard anything about it."

The people sailed away.

Suddenly the old man remembered. "Ahh! I sent those wood chips over there so there would be people on the other side. How could I have forgotten? Why didn't I tell them, when you get there, just don't forget your own language! Speak our Chukchi language. How can I have forgotten?"

"We left in a high wind," they called back. "There was no time to talk. It took us a long time to get there. But birds came to us, gulls, loons. They talked and we understood them. And we began to speak the language of the sea birds. And now we can't talk to you."

"Oh, why did I forget to say?"

Those people came back every year and brought presents. They brought clothing, short jackets, short pants, short boots. All their clothes were short because they were made from wood chips!

And that's my story![9]

This story explains many things—how there got to be people in Alaska, and where their language and clothes came from. "You'd better not tell it over there," laughed Valentina. "They might be offended to know the truth!" The creation of people from wood recalls the image of the tree of life, which the Chukchi may have brought with them on their migration from the south. Some of the peoples of Sakhalin Island to the south have creation stories involving different people's origin in the sap of different trees. And many Amur peoples believe that the souls of unborn children are kept in nests in the tree of life.

That same evening, another guest told a story. She is Antonina Kymytval, a well-known Chukchi poet. Her story is another of those that explains how things came to be. There are many explanations for this particular phe-nomenon, and hers is rather unusual. It may be her own invention. Like Valentina Itevtegina and the well-known Chukchi writer Yuri Rytkheu,[10] Kymytval uses folklore in contemporary settings and styles.

In the past, men frequently had two wives, just as women had two hus-bands. Although it was accepted, this was not always an easy situation. Kymytval tells about it from a more contemporary viewpoint, combining elements of tradition with a humorous sophistication. A more common story about mosquitoes tells of a person throwing an evil monster into the fire, where the sparks leap high, turning into the irritating insects that remind us that the monster was not completely defeated.[11]

Mosquitos

There lived a man and his wife. To tell the truth he was not a very good husband—he was always looking at other women. In fact, he not only looked at them, he brought them into the yaranga and right into the sleeping room!

Meanwhile, the wife prepared food—she cooked, she fed him and sewed his clothes.

One time when he brought another woman home she went up and sat alone on the mountain. She thought, "Why should I go on cooking and sewing for this man?"

And then she got an idea how to get even with him. She took some clay in her hands and formed it into a ball. She made one end a little longer. And then she took some reindeer hair and made a sharp nose. And she formed light wings and gave the mosquito a nasty loud voice. And then she made them many!

She went back to the yaranga. And there was her husband in the bedroom with another woman. She let all the mosquitoes go in there and they began buzzing around and biting the man and the woman.

At first the man thought this new woman had brought the mosquitoes. But the next time he brought someone else, and the same thing happened. And the next.

Finally he thought to ask his wife. Maybe she knew where they were coming from. But when he looked for her she had turned into a mountain sheep and gone away into the mountains.

The Chukchi people understand this story and they never kill the mountain sheep.

But judging from the number of mosquitoes around these days, it is possible that there was not just one bad husband! Valentina Kagievna says there are no mosquitoes in her village. What about yours?

2 / Kanchalan

[Raven] Kuikiniaku was living with his wife, Miti. He made little horns from twigs, tossed them out, and said, "Tomorrow these will be reindeer." Miti took long river stones and said, "Tomorrow these will be herders." Then she took moss, made a little fire and covered it with turf, and said, "Tomorrow there will be a yaranga."

And so it was.

—Koriak legend[1]

Central to Chukchi traditional life is the *yaranga*—a portable dwelling made of reindeer skins, designed and refined over the centuries to withstand low temperatures and high winds and to provide a comfortable living and working space for one or more families. Temperatures vary in different parts of the dwelling to allow for different activities.

The *yaranga* is also central to spiritual life and reflects in microcosm the universe and spiritual geography. Every person and every thing has its place in the dwelling, both in practical terms and in correspondence with cosmology. The *yaranga* is usually oriented with its entrance toward the northeast.[2] Because each direction has a spirit, the placement of things in the house has a relationship to those spirits.[3] The *yaranga* is not completely symmetrical—the more gently sloped side faces into the wind. The chief wind comes from the west. The smokehole is the entrance to the upper world, and the hearth, to the lower world.

Instead of using the portable *yaranga*, shore dwellers, both Chukchi and Yupik, lived in semisubterranean houses. They are no longer in use today,

A reindeer-skin *yaranga*, patched with fabric and plastic, near Kanchalan.
These dwellings are used year-round by reindeer herders.

although members of the older generation describe growing up in them.[4]
The subterranean houses were circular in plan and had an underground
entrance corridor that was used for storage and also served as an air trap,
preventing cold winter air from entering the living space. The corridor also
served as a spiritual middle ground between the home and the outside
world. It was the site of many supernatural occurrences. In the older shore
houses, the jawbone of a whale was used for the central support, while a
shoulder-blade bone closed the summer door, high in the wall. Smoke
exited the house through the hole in a whale vertebra.[5] People were effec-
tively living inside a whale, which must be related to the whale ancestry
hinted at in contemporary folktales.[6] In some subterranean houses the
smokehole was used in summer as an entrance. The importance of the
home is embedded in the Yupik language, which orients many directions
from the reference point of the house, as well as from the shore. In the nineteenth century many Yupik also adopted the Chukchi *yaranga*.

A *vezdekhod,* or all-terrain vehicle. Margarita Takakava is in the center, Alexei Tkalich at right.

When I went to Chukotka in the spring of 1993 I was eager to see a *yaranga,* but of course there are none in the city. To get closer to the land, we went out to the Chuckchi village of Kanchalan by *vezdekhod,* a Caterpillar-like vehicle that bears a family relationship to a tank. The name in Russian means "goes everywhere." It took six hours to get to Kanchalan, over frozen rivers and tundra.

There was little to be seen from inside our *vezdekhod,* since it had no windows. All eleven passengers, including two small children and a woman whose face was heavily lined although she turned out to be only fifty-seven, piled onto plain wooden benches in the back and held on in near darkness as we bumped noisily over the uneven terrain. Soon everyone had shed coats and hats and was gasping for breath, because all the heat from the powerful engine came straight into the cab.

We stopped and got out for a rest. The view was dazzling—great rolling expanses of white with not a tree in sight. The air was crisp and refreshing, the April sky clear blue. Beside the frozen river, bits of grass and a few small bushes were beginning to show. Surprisingly, tundra reminded me of sand dunes—the shocking brightness, the wind, the occasional grasses, the lack of landmarks. Tales came to mind of Raven creating this stark land,[7] of a woman turning into a wolf to go in search of her daughter—maybe just the other side of that hill!

Then one of the passengers demanded, "Will I be home in time for Santa Barbara?" Did she really mean "Santa Barbara," the American television soap opera? She did. And with this abrupt return to the twentieth century, we went on.

Kanchalan is a village of about one thousand that supplies brigades of reindeer herders. After the break-up of the Soviet Union, industries formerly connected with the *kolkhoz* and *sovkhoz* began to be privatized, and many have not survived this transition. Sewing workshops were shut down, and the women joined the modern world by finding themselves the first to be unemployed. The men were faring little better, receiving pay unthinkably low even for Russia—the equivalent of about forty cents a month, or enough to buy one kilo of sugar. The village consisted of small frame houses, a few stores, a community center that was still working in spite of cutbacks, and a large residential school for native children from hundreds of kilometers in all directions. Our hosts from the city discovered one local store that was full of things unavailable in Anadyr—elastic, enamel pots, rubber boots, dish towels. They stocked up.

We stayed at the boarding school. The Soviet government brought two kinds of schools to Chukotka—local village schools and bigger, centralized residential schools. For the most part the village schools have always taught just four grades. Most people in their fifties and sixties today describe learning the Russian language when they started school. The next step was the boarding school (Russian *internat*), attended by older village children and nomadic children of all ages. Native languages were forbidden at the *internat* (although they were later reintroduced as subject matter in some areas), and Russian was enforced for all purposes. Standard curriculum replaced storytelling as the way of delivering messages, and Russian fairy tales replaced traditional Chukchi tales for entertainment. Attending boarding schools was a traumatic experience of leaving the family, learning an unfamiliar language, and eating unhealthy food. On the other hand, many people went on from there to higher education and came back to work in their communities, usually as teachers and doctors. Some speak also of the benefits of being more connected with the outside world through speaking a major world language. Still, the effect of the boarding schools on cultural and family life was devastating. I have talked with no one who remembers them with pleasure.

There were no *yarangas* in sight, but we saw signs that they would soon appear. In summer *yarangas* are ringed all the way around the village, where retired people live. In winter the *yarangas* come down and the people live in houses with central heat. The skin covers are bundled up and the poles stacked, waiting for spring.

Early in the morning I went walking with Margarita Takakava, a Chukchi cultural worker who had come with us. She was actively involved in reviving traditional ways of life, medicine, education, and cooking.

She showed me the places where the *yarangas* were stored, the covers piled neatly and the poles stacked or tied up tipi-style. People were emerging to clear the ground and get the covers ready to put up. When a *yaranga* is in use year-round, the skins are rotated; every year new ones are added at the bottom. By the time a reindeer skin is removed at the top several years later, it is well seasoned with smoke—ready to be used for waterproof pants. Here in Kanchalan the people were simply patching the covers, sometimes with fabric or even plastic.

We came back for breakfast in our shared room at the boarding school, and Margarita told stories she remembered from childhood. She remembered scary tales told at night, and her parents using stories to try to make her behave. She was a tomboy, disobedient and rowdy—and she never did learn to sew. Even then I could see a hint of that child in the easy grace with which she moved in her country clothes—her old trousers and sweaters—as opposed to the shy woman well dressed for work in the city.

I met Margarita first in her office at the House of Culture in Anadyr. Alexei said she was very knowledgeable about traditional culture. That first day she explained the whole cycle of Chukchi holidays to me, but somehow we didn't really relax together in that setting. Her telling had a nervous quality, and my listening did too; it was one of my first experiences recording people's memories on tape, and I felt awkward about asking questions. I even accidentally erased part of that first interview. But the bone-rattling ride in the *vezdekhod* seemed to have shaken that discomfort away—and put her on her own home territory.

Here at the school she told me about how her father cured her toothache by telling stories. She also explained the educational story while we drank tea and ate bread and sausage.

"A proverb comes first—and then the story," she said. "Like this. My father said you must never brag before the event. There was a man who bragged that he would bag a moose and set its leg up in the snow to show his prowess. He went out, and while he was hunting a bear killed him—later friends found *his* leg sticking out of the snow. Don't brag before the event!

"Or another story. We children were told not to make noise at night. One time some children were left alone in the yaranga at night while their parents were away at a party. The children were noisy, although one boy tried to make them quiet down. A big *kelye*, or evil spirit, came to the door. He was too big to get in, but his long tongue flicked around everywhere inside. One by one the kelye gobbled up all the children. Only one boy escaped—the one who had tried to warn the others. He climbed up into the rafters, took a chamber pot, and flung the contents into the kelye's face, driving him away! All those other children were lost. Children, don't make noise at night!"

In Siberian cultures, human beings are believed to have several souls. One of these resides in the bones, both in humans and in animals.[8] The life force can be maintained and renewed by keeping the bones in order.[9] Bones are involved in shamanic initiation. Spirits take the body of the initiate apart bone by bone. If they count one extra, the survivor becomes a shaman, able to heal and predict. That kind of death and rebirth happens in the following story. The spider is a sacred helper who frequently appears in stories, as it does here.[10]

The Skeleton

Three brothers lived together in the tundra. They went hunting, and every time they came home they found things missing. So they kept watch and saw that it was a skeleton doing the stealing. Then as they watched, the skeleton's bones fell away, and underneath, a beautiful girl appeared. They caught her and she married one of the brothers. It turns out that she was a girl who had died but was still able to take human form.

One day two of the brothers went hunting and the third stayed home. While they were gone, he died. Actually, the woman killed him. She put his body up on the shelf that is used for drying skins. When the other brothers asked about him, she said he had gone out. But then one brother found the body. They decided to punish her. They made a deep hole in the ground by the hearth and were going to push her in.

She sat there sewing. A spider came by. The spider is well known as a helper. He said, "When they push you, you'll see a string in front of you. Take hold of it and I'll help you." The brothers pushed her into the hole, she grabbed the string, and the spider took her to the upper world.

Margarita said the interesting thing about this story was that although the second part was well known, hardly anyone remembered that the girl had been a skeleton. It seems that this girl undergoes death and rebirth not once but twice.[11]

Margarita claimed not to be a storyteller, and her tales had a sense of being summarized. Clearly she did not tell them regularly and reached back into childhood memory to find them. There are some that she had made into plays for use in educational programs, but these were not the ones she told me.

Margarita told the next story to illustrate that Raven is not only a trickster (to the *kelye*) but also helpful to people. The tale also explains the existence of stone hitching posts, which are important to herding peoples of the tundra and steppe.[12] Like dwellings, the posts have spiritual as well as practical significance. In vast treeless areas, the hitching post takes the place of the tree of life, connecting the three worlds. The Buriat-Mongol people of the area around Lake Baikal carve hitching posts with three divisions that make this clear. In recent years new posts have been erected at places sacred to various clans. Some of them commemorate powerful shamans of the past. Judging from Margarita's story, it seems that this may have been a custom of the Chukchi and Yupik as well.

Raven, Kelye, and Hare

A kelye is chasing a hare. The hare sees a raven.

"Good, handsome one, help me, hide me!" says the hare. Raven helps: he hides the hare, who may be a woman-sorcerer in disguise.

The kelye arrives. "Hey you, raven, didn't you see a hare?" he says.

"No, but I saw somebody flying away!"

"That's him! Help me fly after him!"

Raven takes the kelye up on his back and flies off. The kelye sees the whole world. Then Raven drops him.

"Oi, my hands, my legs, my eyes," cries the kelye. And he falls headfirst into the snow. Raven and Hare say to the kelye, "You can't run on the earth any more. Who do you want to be?" The kelye wanted to be a stone hitching post.

From then on people have come to him, leaving offerings of beads and food.

"Look," says Raven to Hare, "now you can tie reindeer to those legs sticking up out of the ground!"

The next story is about the leather balls made by the Yupik. I've seen many of them in museums. Made of reindeer skin and a carefully worked white sealskin (*mandarka*), they are always decorated with a sun motif. This tale is related to the Northwest Coast story of how Raven steals the sun, which is hidden in a box.[13] In the North American stories, Raven takes the form of the woman's child in order to deceive her father into letting the sun and stars go—this part is missing in the Asian story.[14]

Theft of the Sun

It was dark on the land. Where had the sun gone? One man, Raven, got on his dog team and rode to the upper world, which, by the way, you can reach from this world if you know where to go. He saw a woman sewing a ball and knew that the sun was inside. The ball was decorated with stars.

Yupik balls in the Anadyr Regional Museum. Made of reindeer skin (brown), treated seal skin (white), and reindeer hair representing the rays of the sun.

She began playing. The ball shone.
Raven caught it and threw the sun and stars back in their places.

I listened to Margarita's stories, still exhilarated by the fresh air outdoors and the sun coming through the window. But I was still thinking about the *yaranga*—we hadn't seen one actually standing. To that end we piled back into the *vezdekhod* and bounced another two hours to find the fifth reindeer brigade, the one based closest to the village. This time I sat in the front and saw the great variety of tundra terrain—rolling smooth hills, grassy areas, steep banks—and ptarmigan winging away out of sight over the hilltop. I remembered stories of people lost in the tundra, wandering for days at a time in fog or storms, sometimes within easy reach of home. My admiration grew for our driver, who could find his way. I'm told that even the village dwellers can't do it, only those with long tundra experience.

At last we arrived at the fifth brigade's camp and saw their reindeer. The herders move seasonally to find pasture for their animals, and it was moving day. There was still no *yaranga* fully standing there—only the central tripod poles. The cover had come down and been packed on its own special sled. The small tripods that form the base of the structure were also gone.

42

A member of the fifth reindeer brigade in traditional clothing, near Kanchalan.

We met Vasily Ivanovich Tayorgin, the proud foreman, with his mother, his aunt, and several coworkers. The men showed us their sleds. There may be as many as ten different kinds—light ones for riding, heavy ones for freight, and others for the poles.

The herders pile up reindeer antlers recently thrown off by new mothers, saving them for the spring holiday called Kilvei, when they play an important part in the rituals. There will be dancing and good food, but the most important moment is when the pile of antlers is moved slightly closer to the *yaranga*, symbolizing increase to the herd.

Women were making tea over the fire that still burned under the tripod. Guests from Canada on moving day didn't faze these cordial people. They made the tea from melted snow. It tasted deliciously burnt and had a few reindeer hairs floating in it. We were delighted by our first meeting with a woman with traditional tattoos on her nose and chin. Her son, Vasily Tayorgin, answered our questions in Russian, since his mother spoke only Chukchi.

43

Vasily Tayorgin's mother in a traditional *kerker*. She has tattoos on her forehead.

"They were done when she was a little girl," he said. "It means she comes from a wealthy family with many reindeer." They all laughed, enjoying the idea of grandmother as wealthy and important.

After tea we got back in the *vezdekhod* and rode over the hill to find the other *yaranga*, which had already been moved and set up. Reindeer require enormous amounts of pasture land, but this time the herders were moving only a few kilometers.

And there it was at last—the *yaranga!*

Nobody knows for sure when the *yaranga* was developed, but it is the perfect dwelling for life in the harsh Arctic climate—warm in winter, insect-free in summer, portable, made from materials that come to hand where very little else is available. Reindeer skins form the cover. Highly prized wooden poles or sometimes whale ribs make the frame. Here above the tree line, wood comes a long distance, traded from the thin forests of the Kolyma

River area to the west and the Kamchatka Peninsula to the south. Sometimes driftwood can be found on the shore.

Yaranga dwellers can cook, work, sleep, and tell stories all in an area no larger than ten meters in diameter. The area under the small tripods is used for storage, and food can be smoked by hanging it under the smokehole.

The *chottagin* is the cold part of the *yaranga*—and the largest part. With a fire going, its temperature is ideal for working. This is the place where women prepare skins, sew, and teach their children, and where men make and repair their tools.

The internal room and the skins used to cover it are called *yoroñi* in Chukchi.[15] The *yoroñi* is built to the height of the tallest person in the house, and a big *yaranga* may have more than one. The floor of the *yoroñi* is made of willow branches and skins. The *yoroñi* is heated with a seal-oil lamp; it takes only fifteen to twenty minutes to get warm. Then, even in winter, people can undress and sleep under lightweight baby reindeer skins.

By morning the *yoroñi* is still warm, but damp from people's breath. Every day the women take the skins outside to air. The moisture freezes and they brush it off.

Before the days of collectivization there were four or five *yaranga*s to a settlement, belonging to brothers or cousins. The youngest son inherited his father's *yaranga*, and the others made new ones. Fire and protector-amulets were brought from the parents' home. The *yaranga* was raised according to ritual. Every piece was fed with fresh reindeer blood to assure health and prosperity in the new location. A branch was raised to the top, representing the tree of life that connects the three worlds of Chukchi cosmology.[16] Although most *yaranga*s stand where there are no trees, this custom shows the importance of spiritual ideas and reveals links with southern Siberian cultures in which the tree of life is central.

Some villages can trace their lineage through one fire as far back as the seventeenth century. The fifth brigade consists of two *yaranga*s, and even after many years of collectivization, most of its members are related.

"Ours is a young family," says Tayorgin's wife, Tatiana. "Our yaranga is four years old." The main cover is made of seventy reindeer skins, and the internal sleeping compartment takes another sixteen. "It's nice to sit here in the sun while the old women are away. When they get here we'll have to work!"

Tatiana Tayorgina, fifth reindeer brigade, near Kanchalan.

The people of the fifth brigade say they live better than those who are farther from the center. Out there the reindeer are less healthy, perhaps from lack of food caused by mining and nuclear contamination. Their numbers are down because of poor health and because poachers—Tatiana calls them wolves—are killing the animals. "They take the meat and hides to town and sell them," she says contemptuously. It is clear to herders which reindeer have been killed by real wolves and which by their human counterparts. Among other things, the herders are distressed by the waste—they find heads on the ground. It is an act of extreme disrespect to waste any part of this vital animal, which provides food, clothing, housing, and transportation.

Just as the *yaranga* is central to human life, so the hearth and fire are central to the *yaranga*. The fire starter board is one of the most important family amulets, and fire is carried to a new home from the old. Besides the centrality of fire to human life, the hearth serves as a gateway to the world below the human one. There are stories about people disappearing into the lower world through the hearth, either on purpose or by deceit. In one tale seven brothers hide their sister in the hearth when danger approaches. And we have already heard Margarita Takakava's tale in which a girl is taken through the hearth to the upper world.

Waldemar Bogoras described air ducts coming from outside to help the fire burn in the *yarangas* of his day. It was his speculation that shamans might have used them to arrange their own spectacular disappearances during ceremonies.[17]

People say that shamans truly disappeared during the persecutions of the Soviet period and that today there are none left. But Margarita had stories to tell from her youth about Chukchi and Yupik shamans.

"At the Naukan Whale holiday there were shaman competitions. They did things like cutting themselves or standing on a knife. My parents told about Dedushka Ilyana, a very powerful shaman. He would have a bucket of plain water brought to him. He beat the water until it rose up and then started catching fish in the bucket! Another time this happened—several babies had died. The shaman threw doll clothes on the fire intended for each of the dead children. The sparks went in the direction of the graves—each to the correct place. This was meant to provide the children with clothing in the next world.

"I'm not sure I believe this one, but I heard of a shaman who filled the yaranga with water and ice!

"Many shamans had the power of hypnosis. They could show a thing and make it appear to be so. People say that my father could make a glass so heavy that you couldn't lift it, and then the next moment make it light again. He said to one person, 'I'm going to kill you.' The man ran but he couldn't open the door. Then my father said, 'I'm just testing you,' and the door opened. I asked more as I got older, but my father died early, so I didn't hear too much. Nobody actually says a person is a shaman, but people know."

Margarita's ambivalence in talking about her father as a shaman is echoed in a more ironic vein by the Yupik artist Galina Tagrina, whose stories appear in chapter 8. In Chukotka, even more than in other parts of Siberia, shamans were not openly spoken of even before the Soviet period, because of the danger of naming the sacred aloud. In the 1930s and later it became additionally dangerous to talk of such things—dangerous not only in the spiritual sense but also in the practical world of politics. Although the climate of 1993 was more open, I noticed that Margarita did not tell these shamanic stories in front of Alexei, whose Orthodox Christian beliefs hold shamanic power to be evil.

She went on to tell about concepts of good and evil. "People believe that evil will return to the doer. Like this: There was a place near Ust-Beloye and Krasnino where now there is an expedition base. It's called Ilmuye, after my grandfather. Fairs were held there—winter sports holidays, trade fairs where they sold fish, meat, everything.

"A very big, strong man called Ilakhtegrynin came out of the tundra to one sports holiday. Nobody could defeat him. And my father, who was about sixteen at the time, jumped on him and that man broke his rib. Later my father got tuberculosis and claimed that this man would be responsible for his death.

"Years later, after I had finished school, worked, then graduated from the institute and worked some more, I was walking one day in Tavaivaam. A woman was coming toward me with a man of about fifty. He was still healthy and strong. I recognized him as that man who had broken my father's rib. He recognized my face and asked, 'Where have I seen that face? Who does she look like?'

"I told him, 'I am Takakava's daughter. You are responsible for my father's death.' He looked very frightened. Then he went quickly on. He must have been eighty but looked fifty. That spring his dogs carried him into the water, through a crack in the ice.

"People believed these things about the return of evil."

On our way back to Kanchalan we stopped for some ice fishing and to watch the herd of reindeer. These were the females and new babies, eating cranberry plants and grasses just showing from under the snow. More antlers were gathered on the ground, waiting for Kilvei. The reindeer moved away as we approached. We kept our distance, not wanting to disturb the mothers and babies. And we admired the venerable profiles so dear to the Chukchi people.

Back in the village, Margarita watched the local ensemble rehearse. She corrected the children's gestures and pronunciation and encouraged them to continue. She was insistent that people use the dialect specific to their own village in performance, and that girls and boys distinguish their pronunciation. Certain sounds in the Chukchi language are pronounced differently by men and women, but in the schools all children are taught to use the male pronunciation.

Bogoras believed that the women's pronunciation was more ancient and was better preserved because women stayed at home more. "They [the women] use in most cases instead of *č* an *s̓*, and instead of *r* [particularly after soft vowels] *š*. They also use instead of *rk* and *čh* the double *šš*. Contracted forms of words are never used by women."[18] Both women and men were capable of pronouncing both sounds and would do so when quoting, but the distinction always remained. Bogoras went on to say that the nomadic Chukchi women worked much harder than men, doing all the work in the home and sometimes taking on men's work in the herds. Men, on the other hand, knew nothing about work in the home and didn't even know the names for all the parts of the *yaranga* and household utensils.

Margarita described her grandmother's consternation when she, Margarita, came back from school talking like a boy! On the other hand, some boys did not go to school but stayed home with their mothers while their fathers were gone for long stints in the army or working away from home. They wound up talking like girls, to the consternation of their fathers. All this is just part of the generational split that exists in language today. In spite of her efforts, Margarita said, when she retained dialect and gender distinctions in her writing for the Chukchi newspaper, her work was edited to meet the standard.

Most linguists agree that the Chukchi and Yupik languages are endangered. When a language dies, a whole view of the world goes with it. The loss of Arctic peoples' ideas about their relationship with their surroundings, nature, and each other is a great tragedy. Language plays an enormous role in a people's sense of self and history.

What specifically will be lost if these languages die? What thoughts become difficult or impossible to express without the original language? Both Chukchi and Yupik are highly specialized for the needs of hunting and herding. Both are rich in ways to describe precise locations, animals of different ages, colors, and genders, conditions and changes of weather. Locations can be described from the orientation of the speaker or of another person or landmark. Language orients to the home, with terms for direction such as "toward the house" and "uphill from the house."

Important in terms of religious views is the concept that hunters do not kill animals but that animals come to people as guests, offering their bodies as food. This is tricky to translate into Russian or English, and translation makes a huge difference in meaning. As foreign terms take over, a young person's idea of what he is doing while hunting changes too. Alexander Omrybkir, head of the Association of Native Peoples of Chukotka, says that hunting and herding are the areas in which language is best preserved today, because of the precision of the native language. In both these occupations, speed and accuracy of communication are of the essence. But this refers to practical matters, not spiritual.

Although it is good to know that language is surviving in this context, I am disturbed and suspicious when what is praised is only that which has to do with that favorite Marxist value—production. Although language connected with work is of the greatest importance, practicality is not its only value. Practical distinctions that are better expressed in the native language are only a small part of the picture.

Storytellers and shamans are concerned with the spiritual power of words—their ability to heal through song and story, to affect the weather, and to express the place of humanity in nature. Such things do not carry well in translation, nor does the poetry—the music—of the language itself. Shamans were known to have a much larger vocabulary than ordinary people. I wonder whether a shamanic invocation would work in a foreign language. Spirits are tied to place; perhaps they are also tied to sound.

Margarita Takakava had done an immense amount to maintain and revive Chukchi culture. Among other things, she had published a book of unique and unusual folktales, a book on Chukchi holidays, and numerous articles. She had also helped others to publish their own stories and traditions, as in Lyubov Uvarovskaya's *Tales from Snezhnoe Village*. She turned tales into plays that are produced in small communities.

There is a tragic footnote to my story of Margarita Takakava. When I returned to Chukotka in September 1994, I learned that this energetic woman in her early fifties had died unexpectedly the week before I arrived. She had gone to visit her father's grave, come home, and quite suddenly become ill. Within a few days she was gone. Her loss is felt keenly by all those who knew her and who care for the preservation of culture and the health of Chukotka's children.

I include here one story each from Takakava's and Uvarovskaya's collections. One is another version of the Raven and Fox story told by Itevtegina, interesting for its different point of view. It shows even more clearly than

Itevtegina's the value of establishing good relationships with spirits. On a more prosaic level, it is important to see what is beautiful in things and people with ugly exteriors. The second story, "The Stone Woman," tells of evil spirits and why a person should not walk in the tundra without a dog. It contains elements of initiation and the motif of miraculous escape and expanding shamanic time known worldwide. Caves as homes of divinity are also a world phenomenon. In Turkic tradition, they unite the earth with the upper world, because they are located on mountains and at the same time are home to the earth goddess.

Kurkyl and Nuteneyut

In one yaranga but in different rooms lived Kurkyl and Nuteneyut. Kurkyl was Raven and Nuteneyut was Fox.

Early one morning Kurkyl went out looking for food. He went far, far away. Finally he saw a frozen lake and went out onto it. He made a hole in the ice, got his fishing pole, and started fishing. The raven sat there a long time, but nothing happened. At last, after noon, he felt a fish on the line. A really big, heavy one! Kurkyl began pulling it out, and suddenly he heard the cry of a child. But this was not a human child, it was a kelye child. He pulled it out. The child cried and shouted, "Quick, take off the hook!"

Raven took off the hook and suddenly loach [a type of carp] came from the child's left side, and from the right, grayling, salmon, and herring. Kurkyl took as many fish as he could, sewed the child up and put it back in the water, and went home.

He came into the yaranga, hid the bag, and went straight into his yoroñi. All the same, Nuteneyut sensed the smell.

"Where is that tasty fish smell coming from?"

"Somewhere," said Kurkyl.

That night the fox couldn't get to sleep. Finally she couldn't stand it: she put on her kerker and quietly went out.[19] She found the tracks and followed them. It was still dark when she came to the lake and started fishing. She got nothing. Only toward evening the line got heavy. She started pulling and had almost pulled it out when she heard the cry.

"This must be where the kelye is hiding the fish!" she guessed, and ran home.

"You're ruining all the best places with your curiosity," said Kurkyl.

Early in the morning next day, Kurkyl went out into the tundra. He went a long way, and it started to get dark. Finally he saw one lone yaranga. He went into the yoroñi, and right away a woman came out. It was so dirty in there that I can't tell you about it, but the raven began to think out loud.

"Where can I have come to? What a big sleeping room, and such cleanliness all around!"

As soon as he said that, a woman came with a big wooden tray. Everything was on that tray—roots, fish, and even wild reindeer meat with green onion. Raven ate the whole thing! When he was full, the woman called him.

"Guest, look at me!"

Kurkyl came out of the yoroñi and saw an ugly woman with messy hair and torn clothing and boots.

"Oh, what a tidy and beautiful woman I'm seeing!" he said.

They began dancing freely, and then the raven wanted to go home. The woman filled his hood with different foods. Raven came home carrying a lot of food and hid it behind the wall.

He came into the sleeping room.

"Where is that tasty meat smell coming from?" asked the fox.

"Yes, it must be coming from somewhere," said the raven.

That night Nuteneyut followed Kurkyl's tracks. She found the yaranga, went into the sleeping room, and began to think out loud.

"Ooh, what a dirty yaranga!"

Hearing this, the woman brought a wooden tray with just a tiny piece of meat and one piece of tundra onion. The fox saw the woman and said, "Although she has lots of meat, this woman is greedy."

"Hey, guest, look at me," called the woman. Nuteneyut came out of the sleeping room and said, "Foo, what kind of woman is this I see? Dirty, messy, in torn clothing!"

The woman heard this and stopped dancing. Nuteneyut came out of the yoroñi and saw just one small mouse, and so the fox came home with nothing. At home Kurkyl said to her, "You're spoiling all the good places with your curiosity."

Early the next morning the raven went off again in search of food. He went a long time and came to a dwelling with no door. He climbed up on the roof, and there was an opening. He looked inside and saw a whole herd of reindeer.

The raven started to think, "How can I shoot one?" and finally he figured it out. He spit at the smallest bull, and the bull died immediately. Raven went down into the house, lifted the bull, and threw it outside. He carried it home and laid it by the wall.

Again Nuteneyut asked, "Kurkyl, where is that good smell coming from?"

"From the place where I was yesterday."

That night the raven decided to follow the fox carefully, but he couldn't help himself and fell asleep. Nuteneyut ran in Kurkyl's tracks. She saw a big dwelling, looked in at the opening on the roof, and saw the herd of reindeer. Beside the wall sat the woman of the house. A big bull went by, and the fox spit on it and killed it.

The woman saw the dead reindeer and threw it outside. "Reindeer are dying," she said.

The fox tried to lift the carcass onto her shoulders without cutting it up, but she couldn't do it.

"Help me with this carcass!" she called.

"I'll be right there. Just close your eyes and wait for me," the woman answered.

The woman came out carrying a stone. "So this is why the reindeer are dying," she thought, and came up to the frowning fox and hit her with all her strength over the head with the rock. The fox fell without even crying out, and the woman carried the reindeer carcass inside.

When the fox came to, the carcass was gone and she had a big bump on her head.

She went home and called to Kurkyl from the door. "You're hiding all the best things from me! Look at my forehead!"

Kurkyl answered, "It's because you're disobedient. I told you I'd always share my food with you."

From that time the fox stopped sneaking out of the house![20]

The Stone Woman

I love the mountains. I love to look at the places where the old settlements were. From these places you can learn about the people; how they lived, their circumstances, their character. First my mother told me, and then other old women told me that you should never walk a long distance alone. Even for a short distance you should take a dog along. Especially young widows were not allowed to go alone, and pregnant women. In earlier times people lived in clans, and this happened maybe ten generations ago.

My mother told me this story. One young widow of about twenty-five, who had two children, often walked alone in the tundra. She wept for her husband and then gathered berries. If there were none, she prepared bark for dying skins. She had four brothers just a little older than she was.

Her old mother tried to protect her from new troubles. She was sorry for her daughter. She scolded her for walking alone in the tundra. Anything could happen, she said. The children were small.

The older one, Kavro, was seven, and he watched his mother in silence. He guessed that she was having a hard time. And when she went far away and stayed a long time, his childish amusements stopped. He could wait for her by the hour. When he asked to go with her the next time, she refused.

"Do you want to gather alder bark with your mother? Do you, a man, want to prepare skins? Go to your uncles and learn reindeer herding," she said.

The young widow was called Koko.

One year spring came especially early. They had not had time to move to the summer grounds while the earth was still frozen. The streams had already started moving. The sun was hurrying nature to a hot summer. Koko's brothers, fearing a drought, moved far away to the north, but that didn't help. It meant the reindeer would get a disease in their hooves. And it meant they had to go still farther, to the snowy mountains where there was water and the reindeer would be healthy.

And so they did. Koko and her older son, Kavro, went with her brothers. Her mother bid Koko goodbye with big tears rolling down her cheeks. "What's happening?" she thought. "It's as if we are parting forever."

According to Chukchi tradition, you do not cry at parting. The herd moved on to the high mountains, called Kelenegytti, which means the devil's mountains. They had been called that for a long time. And did no one ever wonder why?

Even today there are many legends about these mountains. It is said that they are not mountains at all but just the rocky tops, on whose slopes much snow has gathered from the earliest time. This snow never melts. A thick green carpet of tundra is spread around this place. All kinds of berries grow there. The only bad thing is this: midway through a cloudless day, a thick fog can come very suddenly. It covers everything with such a thick blanket that a person cannot see his feet.

The brothers were working in the herd, and Kavro was helping them. The long-legged, big-eyed young reindeer took much of his time, and he didn't ask his mother to take him along berry picking. As always, Koko went by herself. The berries were big, picking them was easy, and the woman stopped only when the thick cloud cover completely surrounded her.

She felt that someone was beside her. She could hear *his* breath. Maybe at arm's length and maybe closer. Koko rubbed her eyes and coughed. Someone touched her. And Koko fell asleep, as if this were the whole reason she had come.

She woke up in half-darkness. It seemed that she was in a yaranga, in the sleeping room. She stretched out her hand. Emptiness. She heard someone moving nearby.

She looked up and saw a kelye. Yes, hairy hands, hairy face and body. The kelye noticed that Koko had woken up, came closer, and placed a finger to its lips. Koko was not afraid. It was as if she had lived there for a long time and had just awakened.

The kelye offered the woman food. There were berries, frozen meat, fish, and something dried. Nothing cooked. And there was no fire to be seen. The kelye was female. This was obvious from the lower part of her body. She had no clothing on. The kelye almost never looked the woman in the face.

Somehow the kelye showed her a storeroom full of supplies. There was no light there either. But if you spend a long time in darkness, you get used to it and start to see as if it were day. Koko fell, and when the kelye helped her to get up she looked her right in the eye.

The eye was human. The eyes spoke but there was no sound. The stone cave that the kelye and Koko were living in was never lighted, and only sometimes, late in the evening, a third someone, big and hairy, moved away the stone that covered the entrance.

When Koko noticed the human eyes of the kelye she started to feel hope. What for? She didn't know herself. She existed as if in a dream, but more and more often, without reason, she approached the kelye woman. The kelye noticed and once stroked her head. From this touch, tears sprang to Koko's eyes.

A long time went by. Koko decided to talk to the kelye. She spoke about her children and her mother, but she couldn't understand her own words. Her tongue had turned to wood. She had great difficulty forming words.

The other one nodded in silence as if she understood. Koko realized that it would be possible to forget her own name. So that this would not happen, she began repeating to herself, "Koko, Kavro."

The time came when the stone moved away from the opening again. The kelye-woman took Koko out to gather berries. There was thick fog, just as there had been all those years ago when *he* took Koko away into his cave.

The kelye told about her own fate, which in many ways resembled Koko's own story. Yes, she too had been human and had been stolen away by that same third someone whom Koko had seen in glimpses. She had forgotten her own name and had grown hair all over. The only thing she remembered was the direction of her native settlement. The kelye-woman could never return there. When she approached, dogs growled. People were afraid of her. They didn't believe that she was human.

The kelye-woman felt sorry for Koko and decided to let her go, before she was completely grown over with hair. She turned her face in the direction of the village and lightly pushed her back. Koko ran and could not feel her legs.

She got to the settlement. Dogs surrounded her, holding onto her ragged clothes. People ran out of their yarangas. Koko repeated two names, moving her lips with difficulty, "Koko, Kavro." Some people could read her lips and passed the words on to others.

A man of about forty came up and said, "Mama has come back. People, this is my mama. Koko has come back!"[21]

3 / Tavaivaam

There were two berries, a cranberry and a blueberry. They got
into a fight—they fought and fought until they burst! The end!"
—Lena Naukeke

One afternoon in Anadyr we went to see a children's ensemble perform for
a group of children visiting from Alaska. The ensemble, neatly costumed in
authentic Chukchi and Koriak attire, performed lively dances, songs, and
even a folktale about a hunter and a bear. After the performance we met
the group's leader, Viktor Tymnev'ye, and asked him to meet us again to
record songs and tell about his work. It is his mother who tells the story
about the berries quoted above. Under her direction the children have performed it.

We got together at the radio studio, hoping that our tape recordings
would be free of the usual background noise. In that large, dark, and totally
silent room, Viktor evoked the world of the reindeer. He demonstrated the
different sounds one can make to call or calm reindeer: there are ways of
calling one animal specifically, without attracting the others, and of waking
a baby without frightening its mother. Viktor was born and brought up
around reindeer and knows them well. His speaking style is that of an
instructor.

"From youth we were taught that the reindeer were the source of our
happiness. They feed us, teach us songs, give us clothing, and much more.

"I was born in 1942 to a family of shore reindeer-breeders. All my relatives and ancestors were herders. I am the only one who has done something
different. Why?

57

Viktor Tymnev'ye demonstrates a traditional Chuckchi dance. Anadyr.

"I, too, began by working with the herds and turned to folklore only at the age of forty. At that time I realized that our traditional beliefs had been suppressed, although my parents continued to do rituals. The lineage of the nomads was broken, mostly by the boarding schools. Not just the fact that children were away from home, but also the program. Everything was European teaching, even the folklore and games. Respect was paid to Russians, not to our own ancestors. This is why the lines are broken. I wanted our children to know their own heritage.

"I remember when I was in the boarding school in 1960. There were some Chukchi books in the attic. Books were printed in the Chukchi language during the early Soviet period and later burned when the emphasis shifted to Russian culture. I used to love to go up there and look at them—I loved to draw the reindeer and the tundra, but it was not allowed. Later I went back to the attic and the books were gone—and around the same time there was an interesting bonfire. . . .

"When I started to work, I turned first to the belief system. I use drawings to explain. The world is in three forms—this physical world with its plants, animals, and people, where each place has a spirit; the upper world, which also has reindeer herding, hunting, and fishing; and the lower world, the sinful world. The connection between these worlds is the polestar. To help a person go straight to the upper world after death, they burned the body. If the weather was good it meant the spirits had accepted the soul; if the weather was bad they had not. The shaman was the one who could go freely between the worlds.[1]

"When my father died I felt a great emptiness, and it was then that I decided to work with children—I wanted to connect that broken line. I went into the kindergarten. Everything there was in Russian, and Russian children were teasing the Chukchi. I taught them Chukchi dances, and that was fine, but they could not relate to the words of the songs—instead of Chukchi words they had been taught Russian words—and for things they had never seen, like fields. So I worked mostly through dances and then later added songs and poems.

"I talked with the grandparents, but much had already been forgotten. Some of what I learned about the old holidays and rituals I read in the works of Bogoras.

"When I was young, I was often sick. Mother went to one old man named Kungang. He said I was sick because the spirit of a baby walrus had come back. Then my mother remembered. While she was pregnant she had been on the shore and felt the pain of a mother walrus. An inexperienced hunter had killed a baby walrus. A good hunter would have killed the mother first, because if you kill the baby first the mother gets very aggressive. In this case the mother walrus was searching for the baby and her pain went into my mother's womb. Once they found out about this past life, things got better for me."

I had a hard time understanding how Viktor's mother's experience related to a past life, but the idea of transmigration of souls gradually became clearer after I met his mother, Lena Naukeke.

Viktor sang many songs—some handed down from his father and other family members, some newly composed by him. When I asked for a story, he told the legend that explains how there came to be an island in the middle of Anadyr Bay. I have noticed that men more often tell historical legends, whereas women tell magic tales. Often this interest has a political basis—the men are searching out history in order to debunk the idea put forward in Soviet times that their people were primitive. In Chukotka, many legends tell about wars over pasture. Victor's legend also shows how a shaman made predictions from his dreams and how conflict arose between those who believed and those who didn't. He told it in Russian.

How There Got to Be an Island in Anadyr Bay

In Anadyr Bay there is one island. Piri-sven is its name. Piri means to catch up quickly, sven—to cut off.

This story is about the time when people couldn't decide who was going to pasture their reindeer where. There was a lot of war among the Koriaks, Chukchi, and Even.

It happened in the spring. All the reindeer herders were moving to their summer camps. The time is called Kit-kit, time of bad weather, with strong frosts. They moved.

There was one young fellow called Vitegyn. He paid close attention to nature and could foretell happenings. At this time, he fell asleep; he slept one day, a second, and a third. His father thought he was going through a prophetic sleep. Others laughed and said he had just got lazy.

Then they came to the summer camp. They made sacrifices so that hunting would be good. The ice was going out. They brought sacrifices to masters of fishing. Vitegyn was still asleep. The men were getting ready to take the reindeer out on their summer route when suddenly he woke up.

He said to his father, "You must take down the yaranga, get dressed in winter clothes, harness two reindeer."

The father told everyone. Many people laughed. They said Vitegyn had slept too much and gone abnormal, that he was crazy from too much sleep.

Others were not so sure. There were a lot of mosquitoes and little to make a raft from. How would they get to the other side? But some believed him; they started to take down the yaranga and dress in winter clothes.

Suddenly it started to snow. The water froze up. Vitegyn said, "Set off, just don't look back, and the herd will come right after you." And so they moved. The whole caravan, people and freight.

At the end of the line was a young woman. The first sleigh got to the other side. This young woman couldn't stand it and looked back. Everything around her began to thaw. On the last sled were the skins for the yoroñi, and they began to fall off the sleigh into the water. She tried to pull the bundle back but it got heavier and heavier. Everybody tried but they couldn't get it out, and at last they cut the ropes and let it go. When they got to the other side they looked back at their old camp and everything was burning. The people who had stayed behind had been killed by enemies.

They looked back at the bay, and that yoroñi and sled had become an island. And from that time on the fighting over pastures stopped.

Soon after our session with Viktor we visited the kindergarten in the Chukchi village of Tavaivaam, which is a half hour's walk from Anadyr. There we were met by children and their teachers—three Valentinas. They came out and greeted us by walking around us burning sweet grasses. This was to remove any evil forces that might have attached themselves to us on the way. Inside we ate reindeer ribs, drank tea, and looked at the artwork these talented children had produced. They were learning to prepare skins in the traditional way, which is far superior to chemical methods, as well as to do beadwork and make fur mosaics. They had built scale models of yarangas and sleighs, and they sang Chukchi songs.

Valentina Rintuv'ye told me about her studies at the Hertzen Institute in St. Petersburg, where she is getting a degree in Chukchi mythology and traditional culture while working with the children in Tavaivaam.

"They would never kill more than needed," she says of her ancestors. "That would be a sin. Our ancestors revered the bear. If a bear was wounded and not killed, that bear would come back in the form of one of your children.

"When a woman gave birth, they would try to find out who had come back—a distant relative? Or someone nearer? There were ways to find out; one involved a protector-animal that would make a sign on the child. This might be one that a parent had bothered in some way. If someone tore the tail off an animal, there would be a sign on the child.

Schoolroom, Tavaivaam. A student is wearing articles of clothing made by students and teachers at the school. In the background a model shows the internal structure of a *yaranga*—the central tripod, smaller tripods holding up the base, and the tipilike top.

"For example, one woman married a Russian. Her baby had some kind of sign on his back. My mama told her to ask her husband if he had bothered somebody in his youth. He remembered that he had pulled the tail off a horse. When they figured it out the sign went away.

"Other children may have marks on their faces, and the grandmothers would figure out what happened. If a relative had drowned and the pregnant girl sat often on the shore of the river, the old people would say that when the child was born it would be a reincarnation of the one who had drowned.

"Even today people still believe that somebody has come back. That's why they continued to teach all these things to children, even when they

Valentina Kalyayo, a teacher at Tavaivaam school. She is conducting a ritual cleansing smudge to greet guests. Her "tattoos" are done with eyebrow
pencil.

were forbidden. They teach the children to beat the drum for healing and to
shamanize.

"The Soviet government put a lot of shamans in prison so they didn't get
to teach anyone. People tell a funny story about one of those shamans. He
hypnotized the guards and put them to sleep. He and his two companions
took the keys and went out. They came back and woke the guards as if
nothing had happened! Those Russians were angry and poured gas over the
shaman to burn him, but it was like water on him!"

The belief in transmigration of souls seems to include two things—the
return of a relative and the mark of some significant event in the life of one
of the parents. This reminiscence led Valya to send some children to invite
one of the grandmothers to come and tell us more. And so it was that I met
Lena Naukeke, Viktor Tymnev'ye's mother. Naukeke is often consulted
about the revival of rituals and is actively involved with the work of her son's

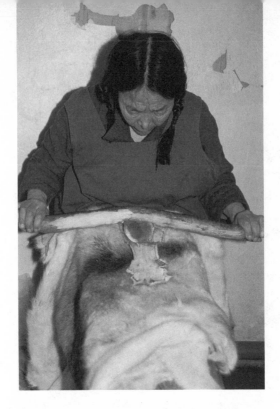

The workshop at Tavaivaam. This woman is scraping a reindeer skin, preparing it to be used for clothing.

ensemble.[2] She is a frequent visitor to this classroom, but it seems that it is unusual for her to be asked about storytelling.

Like the elderly woman we met in the tundra, Naukeke has facial tattoos. "I was probably less than seven years old when it was done," she said. "I don't remember who did it—a woman, but I don't remember who. I do remember that it hurt terribly. She used a needle dipped in coal. There was no thread in the needle. The design is a series of little dots. I had already tried doing it myself earlier, using a needle."

"Did they ever add to them or refresh them afterwards?" I asked.

"Certainly not. It was so painful that once was enough!" So these designs have lasted more than fifty years.

"Why did they do it?"

"Just for beauty. The shore people have different designs from the tundra people, but it is all done for beauty." Naukeke disagreed with the idea that it

The workshop at Tavaivaam. This woman is softening a skin using her feet.

might represent wealth. "People just say that when they don't want to answer any more questions," she said. I wondered if the tattoos were done at puberty as a form of initiation, but Naukeke said that they were not.[3]

She sang one of her personal songs. Each Chukchi might have as many as five personal songs, which are related to his or her childhood name.[4] Naukeke has two, and she also remembers the songs of her two late husbands and her friends. The song she sang was about a person wanting to get warm while moving.

In the past, she said, there were people who could divine the answer to a question using the shoulder blade of a reindeer—they would char the bone in the fire and read the cracks.[5] Others could find answers using the magic mushroom. Certain people can tell who had been reborn in a new baby. Naukeke did not have much formal education, having gone only to evening school. Her parents would not allow her to go to day school, thinking it would spoil her. She could read and write only a little, but she was an encyclopedia of traditional knowledge.

Did she remember a story? She's forgotten a lot, she says, but there is this one. She told it in Chukchi, and Valentina Rintuv'ye translated it into Russian. Although Naukeke speaks some Russian, she is more comfortable telling stories in her own language. This is clearly one of her favorites.

Fish-Egg Face

Brothers—there were a lot of them! The youngest drowned, leaving a small son with his [the drowned man's] mother. The other brothers didn't love the grandmother and grandson, who lived in an earth hut. The grandson went looking for food. But whenever he got something, his uncles took it away.

Grandmother said, "Don't go anywhere, I'm worried about you." But all the same he went out. Once he found a dead seal and put it in a meat hole.[6] But the uncle smelled it and took it away. And they went hungry again.

The boy grew up and started going everywhere in the tundra. One day while he was walking he saw three mounds of earth. One had a little grass, the second even less, and the third was completely bare. From these first two mounds a herd was formed. And from the third, a yaranga. He went into the yaranga that was formed by the mound, and he saw a lot of clothes hanging there, and a sleeping room ready. Everything needed for living. And a herd was pastured around the yaranga.

He went back to his grandmother and said, "Grandmother, let's go home."

"What home?" she said, and began crying. She didn't believe him. He took her up on his shoulders and took her to the yaranga and put her down by the sleeping room.

Only then did she speak. "Whose house is this?"

"Ours," he said. "Come, I'm going to find a bride now. Some rich people live over in the next village. Rub my face with fish eggs so it looks like a beard, and I'll put on old clothes."

They went to the first yaranga in the village. They greeted the people. "Who are you? Why have you come?" asked those people.

They answered, "We're looking for a bride."

The women there said, "No, we won't take a man like you."

They went to the next yaranga. A man, woman, and two daughters lived there. The father asked his daughters, "Who will take this man for a husband?" and the youngest answered, "I will."

"First my grandmother and I will go back to my yaranga," said the boy. There he washed his face and put on good clothes. His grandmother changed clothes, and they went back to the father's yaranga.

They went past the first yaranga, and the girls came out. When they saw how good he looked they said, "He proposed to me first!"

But he said, "I don't want to marry you."

They went to the other yaranga. There he was accepted.

That's all!

Naukeke says she wants to put that story on stage. She gets a big kick out of those rich girls who lost out. She heard the story from her uncle long, long ago. This is one she remembers in its entirety, while others remain only in parts.

The theme of the orphan boy and his grandmother is very common in Chukotka.[7] The boy's uncles should take care of him, and when they do not he often receives supernatural protection. In this case, though, his own ingenuity is enough. In another story similar to this one, the boy turns into a seal to go looking for a wife. Mounds of earth that turn into reindeer and *yaranga*s recall the legend about the creation of the *yaranga*.[8]

The theme of looking for a wife is common all over Siberia. Because most Siberian cultures forbade marriage within one's own clan, a young man sometimes had to go a long way to find a suitable bride. The search might be difficult, and stories about it often resemble tales of a heroic quest or the initiation of a shaman. They also sometimes relate to tales of shamanic healing through the retrieval of a soul stolen by spirits. The idea of making oneself look less desirable in order to test the future bride's worth and perception is typical of Chukotka, although other kinds of deception enter the story in other cultural areas.

Traditional clothing was important not only in providing protection against the elements. As in contemporary life, it also served as a marker of status. Arctic clothing had another level of symbolic significance, since it was made from animal skins. The clothing artist tried, whenever possible, to keep the skin whole and to place it over corresponding body parts, so that a person would be wearing the animal's back on his own back, and so on. In this way, it was believed, people took on the power of the animals that had died to protect and feed them.[9]

Naukeke says people used special words to encourage storytellers, similar to the calls people returned to the shaman during ceremonies. Women and men had different words. Women said, "Hano—kuke—iiii." Men said, "Kak-komei, kotlomei." "Et'rech" is the way a man ends a story. "Etset'" is the women's pronunciation. "Enmen" is the beginning.

Raven and Mice

Enmen! Raven Velkhvin lived with his wife, Miti. Near them lived some mice, and those mice were always looking for lice on his head. One day these mice covered Raven's eyes with a red tie. He fell asleep.

When he woke up he saw red and called out, "Miti, fire! The house is on fire!"

She said, "Take the band off your eyes!"

The mice started searching his head again. Then he fell asleep and the mice came and drew designs on his face like a girl's tattoos. He woke up and went to the stream to get a drink. He saw his reflection and called out, "Miti! Look what a beautiful girl I found! I'll give her this good strap." He went and got it and threw it in the water.

"Take it!" he called. The water washed the strap away. But then he thought, "Of course she won't take it. She's rich and doesn't need goods like that."

Then he threw in the skins from the sleeping room, and the river carried them away. But still she didn't answer, so he said "Take me!" and threw himself in the water.

He called out, "Miti, the clouds are moving so fast!" He was carried to the shore of the estuary.

There he saw many shore birds. He traded heads with them. He went home.

"Where did you get that head?" said Miti.

Then he got sick and pretended to be dead. He said, "If I die, bury me with caviar." Miti laid him in an old earth hut and stayed crying outside.

Up came the red fox and asked, "Why are you crying?"

"My husband died," Miti replied.

"But I saw your husband," said the fox. "He was eating caviar and was all covered with it!"

Then the fox went to the old settlement and pretended to be sick himself. A bear came up and said, "Help me, I'm wounded. A person wounded me, just look at the blood."

Fox had covered himself with alder bark and turned red. "I'm wounded, too," he said.

Bear looked. "Yes, you're covered with blood, too." Bear said, "Heal me." Fox replied, "I'll heat this rock to heal you. Put these heated rocks in the wound." They put heated rocks in the wound, and Bear cried out, "Ow, it hurts!"

Fox said, "Don't worry, this is healing you." And he kept putting the rocks in the wound until the bear died.

The end. Etset'.

Some girls who trick Raven appear in Bogoras's collection in just the same way the mice do in this story.[10] This part of the story is so popular today that I heard it told by an eight-year-old girl in a school in Anadyr. Trading heads with other birds is a familiar raven motif in both Asia and North America. The last part of the tale, where Fox kills Bear with hot rocks, occurs in Northwest Coast tales and also in Bogoras's collection from the late nineteenth century.[11] Similar adventures of Fox and Bear are familiar from the Amur region as well, where Fox convinces Bear to try ice fishing with his tail.

Picking lice from the head is a familiar way of putting a spell on people. Just as bones contain one of the souls, hair is the place where another part of the life-force resides. Playing in the hair while picking lice is equivalent to gaining control over the soul. Combing and braiding one's own hair is a way of raising the soul's power.

The abrupt ending of this story is typical of many tales and is sometimes confusing to Western readers. Several things may contribute to this seeming abruptness, primarily the fact that storytelling in indigenous cultures has a different function from that in European cultures. Over the centuries, Western storytelling has turned into entertainment, especially for children. In indigenous cultures, storytelling has a spiritual and ceremonial function. In describing Native American tradition, Paula Gunn Allen talks about how the literature of her own Laguna Pueblo and Sioux people does not adhere to the unities of time, place, and character accepted by Western tradition. Because indigenous philosophies generally value the group above the individual, and because views of time and space are less rigid than Western ones, a story might range much more freely in these realms while maintaining its integrity.[12]

The ceremonial use of storytelling and the unity of message rather than of time, place, and character bring indigenous story motifs and characters together in ways that may surprise Westerners. Once the message is delivered, the story is finished. As cycles of tales are told and retold, story units recombine, showing various outcomes for a person's actions. In addition to their educational value, sacred stories can heal the listener. Images transform the psyche.

Insiders to the culture will realize that one short story may be part of a longer tale that continues from the point where this episode ends, or simply part of the larger network of tales. The motifs in animal tales in particular go back to the time of creation, and they join up in various ways at different times.

But with oral literature of the former Soviet Union, another factor in story structure comes in. Many tales have been written down over the last hundred years and edited to suit prevalent ideology. In the Soviet period this meant glorifying "the people" and downplaying personal achievement and praise for national heroes. Under the influence of a moralistic boarding-school education, explicit sexual references were also removed. Sometimes today native tellers take tales from books, so that we hear the edited version retold orally. Some stopping points may be arbitrary. While stories have always been changed gradually as they pass from one person to another and as social conditions change, this passing through a written phase, with its conscious ideological focus, is new in this century.

Besides magic and mythical tales, Naukeke also tells legends about the geography of the area. For example, there are three about Mount Dyonis, also called Temel'. In the first, two tribes fought, and their spears broke, giving the meaning "broken sharp things." The second says that two women fought over a needle, and the point broke. In the third, the giant Temel' fought with another ancient giant. The nearest point of the mountain is his head, and the rest is his body.

The idea of divination using the mushroom, which Naukeke brought up, had caught my attention earlier. The mushroom is *Amanita muscaria,* used in many cultures to alter consciousness. The Chukchi say that their own shamans used it for strength, in order to sustain them through long hours of ceremonial singing and drumming. The strongest shamans of all did not use the mushroom.

"The mushroom knows all," says Naukeke. "It can tell the future. Ancestors teach through the mushroom. My grandfather tried it and predicted an earthquake. Soon afterward we heard about the earthquake in Armenia. Mushrooms used to give a person strength. If you ate mushrooms you could go a long time without needing to drink or eat. Reindeer would take off after the mushrooms like beads rolling away. It is so strong it can grow through a rock. Only old people were allowed to use it—young folks could not.

"And then came the legends! Shamans would use mushrooms to give them strength to drum a long time. It's not like alcohol, there's no headache. You get the feeling of being off in the past or future.

"Never cut the mushroom with a knife. One man cut one with a knife, and after he ate it he always had a pain, as if somebody was cutting him with a knife. As if the mushroom itself was speaking, saying, 'They're cutting me with a knife.' Don't cut off the white spots, either. Two people in fifth brigade cut one in two and each took half. From then on they always wanted to be next to each other!"

Our last day in Anadyr we went back to Tavaivaam to celebrate Kilvei, the spring reindeer holiday. A *yaranga* had been raised in the street and a reindeer slaughtered for the occasion. There was dancing and singing, boiled reindeer meat and pancakes. Viktor piled the reindeer antlers carefully, and then Naukeke and Valentina corrected him. I watched closely for the moment when the antlers were moved closer to the *yaranga* to ensure a good year to come. This subtle movement, much smaller than the dramatic dances being performed, is the heart of the holiday, showing the people's intention that reindeer will come ever closer to the *yaranga*.

I tried a drink of reindeer blood, feeling a surge of hot energy course through my body. Grandmother Naukeke brought me the skin of a baby reindeer as a gift, and we all said goodbye. It felt as if we had been in Anadyr a long time in that month and that we had good friends there now.

The next day we rode to the airport in a military truck. The season was risky—the airport is on the other side of the bay, which was almost thawed. We had been hearing loud, booming cracks as the ice started to break. City buses had stopped running across the ice, but cars and trucks were still

Lena Naukeke adding a reindeer antler to the ceremonial pile at the Kilvei rituals. Tavaivaam.

going. In summer there is a ferry, but during this season in between, travel is risky. Our truck sloshed through what seemed like lakes and rivers on top of the ice. From the windows we could see big cracks. Our Russian friends were talking very fast, nervously ignoring what was happening outside the windows.

Suddenly, when it seemed we had almost made it, the truck crashed heavily to one side. Sure enough, one wheel had gone deeply into a crack in the ice. Our door was jammed shut. The driver got out and sloshed through the freezing water—no, there was no way he could drive out.

We waited nervously, counting the time until our plane was scheduled to leave, wondering if we would have to get out through the roof opening and walk through freezing water up to our knees. And then, as suddenly as this little adventure began, it was over. A truck designed for water delivery pulled up, our driver quickly attached his chain, and instantly we were upright again. Off to the airport.

Victor Tymnev'ye and Valentina Rintuv'ye making a sacrifice to the fire at the Kilvei celebration. Tavaivaam.

We needn't have worried about missing the plane. True to form, it was eight hours late. We found a television in the airport building and watched the local news. Much to our surprise, we saw ourselves—at Kilvei in Tavaivaam!

4 / Providenia

Every place has its spirit, which can help you or harm you. You
must bring an offering to that spirit. We always feed the spirits.
We give a little bit of whatever we have, whenever we go out.

—Lyuba Kutylina

In September 1994 I flew to the town of Providenia, on the Bering Strait.
There I hoped to get acquainted with the stories of the Siberian Yupik, who
live in several villages not far from the town. I came alone this time, flying
from Nome, Alaska, in a plane that held about ten people. That day there
were only four passengers—the other three were on a trip to study whales
and walrus and the possibilities of eco-tourism in the area. The flight took
only an hour and a half, and it was fascinating to see the shore of North
America give way so quickly to the shore of Asia. We flew along a fjord with
cliffs on both sides and arrived at a small airport. We could see the town on
the other side of the bay.

We came through customs without incident. When we emerged, people
were waiting for my three fellow passengers, but no one was there for me. A
bus pulled up, quickly unloaded, reloaded, and left again. Still no one. What
could have happened to Svetlana? I had written the exact time of my arrival
well in advance and had it hand-delivered by the airline's agent. Why did no
one meet me? I felt terrified.

I decided my best bet was to tag along with the others, so I begged a ride
to town, which the Russian guide grudgingly allowed. On the way I asked if
he knew my friend Svetlana, and he said he was sure he had seen her flying

away to Anadyr the week before. This sounded bad. She was the one who knew all the people here. Without her I would be lost.

We bounced along the dusty dirt highway that skirts two sides of Providenia Bay and came into town. A bare black mountain rose above us to a sharp point. It looked man-made, but it is not. In the old days people did not live on that side, I learned, precisely because the land seemed dead.

Like many a provincial town in Russia, Providenia looked as if it had been bombed—the streets and sidewalks were rubble, the buildings dilapidated. Nothing seemed to be open except the bar. The driver took us to a dormitory where sailors stay—Providenia has no hotel—and from there I called Svetlana's friend Irina, whose number I had been given.

"Why didn't you write?" she screeched. Aha, my last message had not come through. Because the postal service is so bad, and telephone impossible, I had mailed my note on a pretty photo card through an agent. Perhaps the pretty photo was a mistake—there are people in Russia who will sell anything.

Irina calmed down and came over to get me with her big dog, Ralph. Nothing in Providenia is far from anything else; it was an easy walk back to her apartment in the newest building in town.

Soon I was seated in her kitchen eating borsch. After a while Svetlana showed up, angry because she had waited a long time for me to arrive. She had been in Providenia to teach a course earlier in the summer, and, because she couldn't afford to fly home and then back again, had simply waited the extra month. Now it seemed that not one but two of my letters had failed to arrive. She didn't know that I had been busy all summer and unable to come earlier.

She waited while I finished a second bowl of borsch and then said we should go over to the Providenia Regional Museum and meet the people there, who would help me during my month in Providenia. These workers were warm, knowledgeable, and helpful, going out of their way to introduce me to interesting people and to arrange transportation to villages. Without Alla Panaug'ye, Alexandra Sokolovskaya, and Vladimir Bychkov, the director, who gave his blessing to my project, very little would have been accomplished.

We were still talking about producing a photograph album on Chukotka.

The previous year Svetlana, her husband, Alexei, my husband, Murray, and I had played with the idea of an album showing Chukotka at the different seasons, or one showing all the regions. The Department of Culture had given its approval to the project, but it seemed impossible to carry out, given the difficulties of transportation.

We then settled on the idea of an album about the arts and crafts of Chukotka, this being Svetlana's specialty. By now our four were reduced to two —Alexei was busy teaching, and Murray and I could afford only one airline ticket. I became the photographer.

We were still going on this second idea about arts and crafts when I arrived in Providenia, although I had begun to suspect that it would not work either. Craftwork is not my specialty, nor do I have skills for photographing artwork. Add to this the fact that craftspeople experience tremendous difficulties in Chukotka getting quality materials, along with the difficulties involved in my traveling to see them, and it was hard to see how I could produce that kind of book. Instead, I suspected, it would probably focus on stories, although this did not especially interest Svetlana. In retrospect, the Chukotka project has been a painful lesson in appreciating what is and relinquishing control over what is not. But I certainly did not have this philosophical attitude at the time. I was worried about my obligation to the Chukotka Department of Culture.

We went to the museum, a small building located in the center of town next to the coal-fired electric plant. Seeing the exhibits was quickly accomplished. They were all housed in two small rooms, showing plants and animals, archaeological finds, and traditional clothing and household goods of the Yupik and Chukchi. A small exhibit showed Russian settlement of Chukotka and artifacts of the great October Revolution. Another, larger room was devoted to special exhibits, at the moment a collection of paintings by a local artist whose work caught the particular light of the Arctic tundra especially well.

By the end of my visit to Providenia, the museum was moving to a newer and more spacious building where the staff would be able to display much more of their interesting collection.

That day a young Chukchi woman named Svetlana Chuklinova was visiting from Anadyr. She works with Ergyron, the prominent Chukchi dance ensemble, but she comes originally from Nunligran, a village of about five

Svetlana Chuklinova, a Chukchi teacher and performing artist with the well-known ensemble Ergyron.

hundred on the coast of the Bering Sea in the Providenia region. One of the museum workers was her favorite teacher back in elementary school, and she had dropped in for a chat. She agreed to show me some dances and songs, so I rushed home and came back with a video camera.

We went alone to the special exhibits room, which has few visitors. Svetlana shrugged out of her jacket, exposing an Adidas T-shirt and jeans. In her early thirties, Svetlana speaks Russian as her mother tongue—she says the elders complain that her Chukchi is not very good. But now she is actively involved in cultural activities. Like Viktor Tymnev'ye, she consults with the elders and then teaches children the traditions of their ancestors.

"My Chukchi name is Givintegreu," she says, "which means 'The new year coming on the shore,' and Ettyrakhtina, 'The dog came back.' This means our dog died the night I was born. I was born and raised in Nunligran, where I learned sewing from one aunt and singing from another. My grandfather was a shaman. He prayed to the sun or to a star at night. He healed with the drum. They were never called 'shaman'—people simply knew. He didn't accept any pay for his work. He also hunted sea animals and traded for reindeer meat and skins, which were vital for clothing. I was born in a yaranga, but since my father was one of the first in the village to get an education—he became a bookkeeper—we soon got a wooden house. Now everybody has them.

"The summer yaranga cover was made of walrus skin that let a lovely light through. There were beautiful smells in a yaranga. People worked together quietly to put it up—everybody knew how.

"I had a traditional upbringing. For example, we were taught not to go out in the evening. When people sit down to eat, the women have prepared all the food while the men sit outside the room somewhere discussing communal matters, like building a boat or yaranga. Then everyone comes and sits in a circle. You must respect your elders. No one starts to eat before the man of the house. Parents told the children to keep quiet around elders. Even if they are wrong, we were told not to say anything, just to listen and go our own way.

"I've just been several days in Nunligran now, and I've eaten so much! Everywhere you go you must drink tea, even if you don't eat. It would be offensive to refuse. It would mean you are greedy, that if this person were to visit you, you don't want to return the favor. Grandma said, 'If a guest comes, always feed him first, even if it is an enemy. After food you may ask why he came.' This is why guests think the Chukchi drink a lot of tea!"

Svetlana sang a song about a crane and a girl whose young man has left her. Girlfriends get together and appeal to the crane to take the boy a message asking him to come back. Svetlana sang another song about girls dressing to go dancing. Several of her songs display the Chukchi art of throat singing. Different from the throat singing of the Inuit and of Central Asia, it seems to imitate the sound of the reindeer, with intense sounds produced on both the in breath and the out breath. Svetlana does this singing better than anyone else I've heard, producing fascinating sounds along with intensely changing facial expressions and gestures.

These songs have been arranged for the stage. The use of performance is a major part of cultural renewal in many parts of Siberia. Today's ensembles have emerged from those formed during the Soviet period, but there has been a shift of emphasis over the past few years. Whereas the old ensemble performances were highly choreographed and devoid of spiritual content, now more elements of ritual are being added. There is a greater sense that these performances carry the voice of tradition and are vital to the education of young people. Many young people are working with tremendous dedication, seeing performance as a vehicle for preservation of identity.

"We ran a Chukchi week in December with the children," said Svetlana. "We had a day of poems, others for songs, stories, competitions in art, dance, and in gathering memories from their elders. The final winners were presented to the whole village.

"When I'm dry on ideas, I always go to the elders. Of course they told stories. I heard so many I don't always remember who told which one.

"One thing you must never do in storytelling is to imitate the raven exactly. It will bring bad things. Also, don't make jokes about the bear, or he'll get after you. The bear and the raven are sacred. I had one grandmother whose name had something to do with bringing in berries—she made sacrifices to a bear skull.

"When I asked too many 'why?' questions, like 'Why did they make sacrifices to the bear?' the elders would say, 'It will all come in its own time.' You shouldn't talk about contact with spirits."

Here is a story Svetlana told about a bear, expanding the theme of reverence for the animal. Her story praises the values of the tundra—the man's care for his family and his ultimate refusal to give up. Svetlana heard it from her mother, Nineut. She tells it now to children in Russian.

The Man Who Wintered in a Bear's Den

They say this really happened, long, long ago. In one village there lived a man with his wife and children. They were very poor, and he worked as a herdsman for some rich reindeer breeders. The master was very strict, but in spite of that he paid something, and the people managed to get by. They didn't die of hunger, but at the same time they didn't live well.

The man reasoned to himself, "The more I work, the more the master will pay me." So he was rarely at home, always out with the herds. One day he went out to pasture the reindeer as usual.

He was out working this day when a terrible storm came up, with very strong winds. The reindeer ran off in different directions. No matter how he chased them he couldn't gather them together, and the wind beat him so hard that at last he fell to the ground, exhausted. He lost consciousness. When he came to, all the reindeer were gone.

"If I go back without the reindeer, the master will kill me," he thought. "And if I die in shame, my wife and children will die, too. Better for me to go off into the tundra. Maybe I'll find the reindeer there. At least if I die in the tundra, people will take care of my family."

And off he went.

"Death waits for me," he thought.

But suddenly he fell! It was all dark; he couldn't see anything. "Maybe I fell into a hole," he thought. He looked around, and there he saw a bear! Not only a bear, but a female bear—with a baby! Everyone knows that if a mother bear sees a human near her cub she will rip him to pieces.

"Now she will kill me," he thought. He got ready to die—he lay down and closed his eyes. But then he thought, "Why should I die like this? I might as well accept it."

He sat calmly.

The mother bear was sleeping. She opened one eye and looked at him. She was still asleep.

"If I move," he thought, "she will attack." He sat without moving for a long time. At last it got painful and cold.

He opened one eye. He moved one toe.

The bear opened one eye and closed it again.

Then he tried moving his foot.

Again she opened one eye and closed it.

"If she hasn't attacked yet, maybe I can move my foot a little more," he thought.

He moved, and she opened her eyes and gave him a strange look. Was it the look of a friend or an enemy? She looked at him a long time, then turned her head away and lay down to sleep.

"If she hasn't attacked," he thought, "it means maybe I can move my arm."

And so it went. He stayed there in the den for a long time, moving only a very little.

He got very hungry. There was some meat in the corner and it looked really good. But he was scared of the bear.

"Oh, if only I had something to eat!" he thought, looking at the meat.

The bear opened her eye. She looked at him and she looked at the meat. And then she took a piece with her paw and threw it to him!

He took the meat and ate it. Then he sat there longer. He stayed there for several days, living in the bear's den. Then he got a little braver and walked around in his corner. He didn't come close to the bear or the cub.

He started to think, "I have to get out of here somehow. He had with him a *teviskhin,* made of reindeer antler for beating snow out of fur clothing. If he could put the teviskhin over the top of the hole, he could pull himself out. But to do that he would have to stand on the bear! What to do? He thought and thought and thought!

Then she opened her eye, got up, and moved right under the hole!

"If she hasn't hurt me and has even given me a piece of meat, it means she is well disposed to me," he thought. "If I haven't died yet, it means death is not fated for me now. Whatever will happen, let it be!" And he got up on the bear's back, got the teviskhin out across the top of the hole, grabbed hold, and jumped out!

The bear looked at him, wrapped herself around the baby, and went back to sleep. He said, "Thank you, bear, that you didn't let me die and you saved me from starving."

He started home, thinking, "If I didn't die here maybe I won't die back in the village either. Let the master do what he likes with me."

He went back to the village. People looked at him in amazement, as if he were a vision. "You were gone so long! Where have you been?"

"The bear saved me," he said, and told the whole story.

In several of our villages they worship the bear as a sacred animal. When people found out that the female bear had saved him, had even fed him, they all respected him. He started to live well.

In the spring, when the Kilvei holiday came, he killed several white reindeer and took them as a gift to the place where the bear lived.

They say of this story that good is paid back with good.

Svetlana's telling had a tremendous presence, as if the story had really happened—and to someone she knew. I asked, and she said yes, it was supposed to have happened. Like Margarita Takakava, Svetlana emphasizes the moral of the story. Her telling is that of a performing storyteller, and she draws out the man's holding still to a point of great tension. In retrospect, the story follows the pattern of initiatory death and rebirth. This does not necessarily mean that the man became a shaman, but his life story followed that path. It is a sign of respect to tell a person's life in this way.

Conversation continued, to the sound of a computer game being played in the next room. Perhaps the closeness of death in the bear story brought on thoughts of birth and death. Svetlana began talking about traditions connected with both.

"A pregnant woman ate alone," she says, "on her own dishes. Other people brought her the first of the sea cabbage, full of vitamins. A new child was not shown to anybody but the husband and his family. When I asked why, I got the feeling that was one of those things I would learn in my own time. Guests would all bring gifts for the mother and baby. While pregnant, you should get up early every day and throw a little grain out the door. This will help the movement of the child. Do it before others wake up.

"If someone died and you were the only one to see it, you must report it immediately to the nearest yaranga. You say that the person went away. Two people will come together with a teviskhin to bring the body home. Then you tell everybody. People come, each bringing something to eat. The body is laid with the feet to the door, with the sharpening stone on his chest. This prevents him from waking up again.

"People make special clothes for their own funerals. If there are none when the person dies, they use holiday clothes. You sit next to the body and cry or not as you feel inclined. People laugh and tell stories about the person. Food is prepared. This can last several days.

"If the person was old or died of infectious disease, they buried him right away. Men are buried with toy hunting tools, a woman with all her things, her teacup, needles, sewing things. They set a dish upside down next to the body—a little piece of everything the guests bring goes there. Speak softly, feed all the guests. Later the women must weep together. They pick a leader, the most respected, usually an elder.

"They cover the dead person's face and tie the cover with the lasso. They take food to the place where the burial is to be. In the old days, people used to leave the body exposed out on a hill, after eating and drinking there together.

"Before going out there, they ask the dead person questions. A beater or an ordinary stick is placed under his head. If it is easy to lift, it means yes— if hard, no. Usually a pregnant woman will not go to this ceremony, although I did for my grandfather. We asked where to bury him, when to celebrate, who was to kill the sacrificial reindeer, how many reindeer, and whether he was offended with anyone.

"The leader then goes to the right place. All present circle around the body in the direction of the sun. Next they do a turn or side somersault, rolling over the body without touching it, and go away without looking back. We ask him to leave the relatives in peace. Meanwhile, those left in the yaranga are eating and drinking tea. Women prepare the food, of course. When the people come back, a fire is lit outside the yaranga. Those coming back leap over the fire to cleanse themselves from the spirit.[1]

"They cut the lasso up, and everyone takes a piece home and hangs it up. When we need to, we feed it. The dead person's belt and strap are hung up and fed at every mealtime until the celebration. Then it is taken down, and I have not yet been told what happens to it. We do visit the grave after this.

"Our elders get messages in dreams. In general, it is not a good idea to tell dreams to anyone. Maybe later in life. If you tell them it weakens the gift. I have visions in dreams of what will happen and often go and warn people."

Svetlana showed me a special type of throat singing with movement that is done only in Nunligran. It is about the ritual of starting the fire—the sound and action of the fire-starter board. On the board there is a stick standing upright. It is twirled, using a string, and it ignites a spark in the dried grasses at its base. Svetlana's song imitates the sounds of bringing up a spark.

She sings a very funny one about gossip, and then a song about a one-eyed devil. Women sang this song together, she says. I can hear the word *kokhotain* in the song, or perhaps *kookhlain*, which Svetlana says means one-eyed. I'm especially interested in this song because of my fascination with stories about one-eyed monsters, from the Cyclops in Greece to the one-eyed Shulbus of the Turkic Tuvan people near the border of Mongolia and the one-eyed Barusi of the Siberian Taimyr Peninsula. The Siberian monsters are related to deities and to the spirits called by shamans. There is no contradiction in the idea that a monster can be a spirit helper. Chukchi

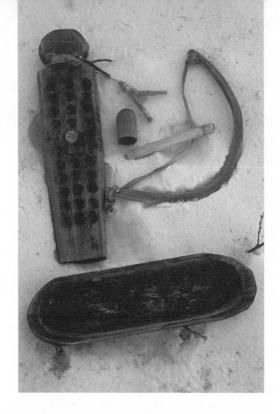

A Chukchi fire-starter board. Collection of Svetlana and Alexei Tkalich.

philosophy is not dualistic, and there is a clear recognition that what is helpful in one situation may be harmful in another. A difficult experience, like that of the man who wintered in the bear's den, can lead to a transformation and to new strength.

I asked if Svetlana knew any stories about one-eyed monsters. Following is the story she told. It is reminiscent of a story widely told on the Northwest Coast about a wild cannibal woman with a basket who takes children away. In some versions she is the one who turns into mosquitoes when thrown into the fire by some clever children. The story resonates with tales from many other parts of the world, including the Russian story of Vasilisa the Beautiful, which may have cross-pollinated with this one when Russian tales came to Chukotka. The motif of magic or "obstacle" flight, in which a person throws a sacred object out behind that turns into an obstacle for the pursuer, is familiar all over the world. A hero who uses obstacles and ritual actions to escape also creates landforms that are familiar to insiders who hear the story.

Six Girls and the Giant

In one family there were only girls. There were six of them, and one day they went out for berries. They picked and picked, all day long. One of them, the youngest, was so bold, she kept going farther and farther away from the others.

The oldest one called, "Time to go home, it's getting late." In the old days, and even when I was little, people used to say, "Don't go outside at night. Koushainin, the evil spirit, will catch you. Or as some other people say, the kelkh."

The older girls couldn't go home without their sister, but she kept going farther and farther away from them. They would catch up, and she would run away. And so they went deep into the tundra and got lost. It got dark.

They heard a sound as if the earth were shaking. What could it be? They fell to the ground and froze there in terror. The earth shook harder, and they heard a loud "boom, boom" coming closer. And then suddenly it got quiet, and they heard the sound of the wind—"whoo, whoo." And again the wind.

Then they heard a loud voice. "Aha, you thought you could hide from me, but I see you." It was the kelkh. She was a big, terrifying woman. And so dirty! She said, "Now I have found good food for myself. I'll put you in my bag and take you to my yaranga." She opened her big, smelly sack, made of old skin, and put the six girls in it. She wrapped them up, tied the bag shut, and carried them away.

The giant woman hung the sack up on a big cliff by the seashore. "Now I'm tired," she said. "I came such a long way, now I'll sleep a bit. And you just stay there. When I've had enough sleep, I'll eat you up!"

The girls were scared. They cried. But the oldest girl had a knife with her. This was the way it was, before—girls and boys, as soon as they were getting grown up, had knives. They had to. She started to cut a way out of the sack.

The girls listened to see if the giant was asleep.

Was she snoring?

No.

They listened again.

Was she snoring?

No.

Still she was not asleep.

They listened again, and this time she was asleep. The whole cliff was shaking from her snoring!

The oldest girl coughed to see whether the kelkh was really asleep. There was no movement from the sleeping giant.

The girl coughed again.

Still asleep.

"Help me," she said to her sisters. "We'll all cough together." They all coughed, and still the giant did not wake up. They coughed again.

They were safe.

Then the oldest got out of the bag. She helped the others, counting one, two, three, four, five . . . and then the kelkh woke up! The girls were scared and ran, leaving the youngest behind. She was sleeping in the sack. The kelkh woke up, and the girl was still sleeping sweetly.

The kelkh thought, "Good, now I will eat. There are six girls in my bag." She came up to the bag and opened it. There she saw only one girl.

"Where are the others?" she shouted, taking the girl by the hair.

"Stop, you are hurting me. I was asleep."

"I am going to punish you," said the giant, and took the girl into her yaranga.

"Don't try to run, you don't know the way. And when I get back, I want everything to be clean and tidy. Fill the pot with water, ready for food. Get in firewood."

The girl was small and the yaranga was very big. The kelkh went away. The girl thought, "How will I do it? I'm just little." She would have to haul the water into the yaranga.

"No, better to run away," she thought.

But as soon as she got out the door she heard a voice: "I see you. Don't run."

The girl thought, "She's gone far away and still she sees me! I'd better not run." So she went back in. But still, how was she to clean up all this mess? Water was needed too.

"I'll run," thought the little girl, "and if she sees me and eats me up, so what?"

But no sooner did she open the door, getting ready to leave, than she heard, "I see you. Don't run. Go back inside."

The girl thought, "She's gone still farther and still she sees me." And she went back in.

Of course the kelkh had not gone away but was standing behind the yaranga, watching.

So the girl had to work. Now I have to tell you that at home this girl was the smallest, the most spoiled, and the laziest. And now for the first time, without her parents or her sisters, she did it all! She cleaned everything up, brought in water, prepared firewood.

Then she thought, "I'm hungry. If only I had a little piece of food." She was so hungry that she fell asleep.

The kelkh came home bringing a whole reindeer carcass. "Are you home?" she shouted.

The girl ran out to meet her. "I'm here."

"Fine, take this reindeer and cut it up."

Now this girl had never before cut up a reindeer and didn't know how. She had never cooked meat. But still she did it. She cut her fingers and got worn out, but she cut up the meat, got the fire going, and cooked meat for the first time.

The kelkh said, "I see that you have put things in order here and cooked food. I will reward you." And she gave her a tiny piece of meat. The girl was so tired that she didn't even have the strength to eat the meat. She fell asleep again.

When she woke up the giant was gone. The girl sat and thought, "How will I get away from this kelkh?" She took the piece of meat and was about to eat it when suddenly a little mouse appeared.

"Little girl, give me a piece of meat."

"No, I want to eat it myself."

"I'll help you to get away from this house."

"Really?"

"Really."

The girl gave the meat to the mouse. "Now come with me," said the mouse.

"How can I get away following you? You're so small, we'll be slow."

"Just try to follow me," said the mouse and off she ran. The girl ran after her. And just then she heard thunder! "Oh no, it's the kelkh. She knows that I ran away from the yaranga. She's probably catching up with us."

"Don't worry. I'll help you." The mouse ran on. She pulled her tail along the ground, and behind her a big ravine appeared.

"By the time she gets across that we'll get away."

Off they went. Again the girl couldn't keep up with the mouse. Again they heard thunder. "It means the kelkh got across the ravine and is catching up with us."

"Don't worry, I'll think of something," said the mouse, and swept with her tail like a broom behind her. Suddenly a big, wide river appeared.

They ran on and finally saw the girl's home. The girl was very happy. "Come home with me. I'll tell my parents that you helped me," she said to the mouse.

"No, your place is here and my place is there. Everyone must know their own place."

The girl came home. Her parents were happy to see her, and so were her sisters. And she said, "I won't be lazy any more. Now I know how to do everything." And she became a good helper in the home.

When she told her family about the mouse, they said, "Mouse may be small but she did a big job!"

The most complete collection of folktales of Chukotka in the Soviet period was made by the linguist-folklorist E. M. Menovshchikov, who taught in the school at Sireniki in the 1930s and collected tales and linguistic data at old Chaplino from the 1940s until the 1970s, from young and old alike. Whereas many editions of tales published in the Soviet era were heavily edited not only for style but for content, Menovshchikov produced several volumes remarkably free of ideology. And while other editions reflect the changing tides of ideological thought in the Soviet Union, in both their presentation and their selection, his are comprehensive. His version of this tale, told by Itkhutkak, was called "Five Girls and Maiyrakhpak."

There are several major differences between Menovshchikov's and Svetlana's versions. In his, the giant calls to a tree to bend down so she can hang her bag up before falling asleep. The girls call first to Bear, then to Raven, and at last to a passing fox for help. The first two refuse, because humans have not treated them well, but the tricky fox calls to the tree to bend down so the girls can escape.

While working in the giant's house, the youngest girl convinces the giant to let her go outdoors for a while. The giant agrees but ties her to the *yaranga*. Since Maiyrakhpak has burned the girl's clothes, she wears the giant's. On the shore she sees two young men, who untie her. Because her finger was cut (while still in the bag), she now has magic, the magic of menstrual blood. She touches a stone with that finger and it becomes a tall cliff; she draws a line on the ground that becomes a river.[2] The giant drinks all the water in order to cross, and her belly swells up. The girl tells her to dance, the belly bursts open, and metal objects come out—teapots, cups, plates, buckets. This is how people acquired metal things.[3]

This last part is often heard incorporated into other stories in the north, explaining where metal objects came from. The earlier episode in which two animals refuse to help but the fox agrees is also common all over Siberia, as are escapes involving the creation of cliffs and rivers.

This is clearly a story about female power and its source. Full of birth images—the sack, the monster's belly—it also shows the girl's magic, contained in the blood, and the importance of helpers. While Svetlana's version emphasizes socializing factors—learning to cook and clean—it retains the essentials of this female initiation.

5 / Chaplino I

A hunter drowned over on the other side, opposite Chaplino.
All the hunters fed the spirit of that place, but this one didn't.
The others told him he should too, but he said, "No, when I was
here in the winter I fed them and they didn't help me. This year
I won't feed them."

Then a seal appeared. That man shot and killed it. He went
out in the boat to bring it back. The others weren't looking
because they were preparing the teapots.

Suddenly the oldest one cried, "Look!" They looked and
they didn't see him. The boat was overturned. When they got to
him he was dead. So, because of that, we are afraid of the spirits.

—Lyuba Kutylina

After my successful first day at the Providenia Regional Museum, I returned
to talk with Vladimir Bychkov, the director. Although he was interested in
my project, it was a very busy time. A couple of days later he was unexpectedly called out of town and was gone the rest of the time I was in Providenia.
But before we parted company he gave permission for one of the museum
workers to accompany me to the village of New Chaplino for the day. Buses
ran there from Providenia on Saturdays.

Alla Panaug'ye's eyes were bright as she agreed to go. She comes from
Chaplino herself and has lots of relatives there. It's always a pleasure for her
to visit the village, she says. Alla was probably in her late twenties, lively and
talkative. As we got to know each other better I learned that she is Yupik,
with relatives in Sireniki village as well. Her mother is Ainana, a well-known

Yupik writer and activist working for the rights of native people in Chukotka and in conjunction with other peoples of the circumpolar north.

We agreed to meet at the bus stop on Saturday morning. Svetlana Tkalich was coming too, to see some of the artists she has worked with. The morning dawned cold, rainy, and windy. September in Providenia means that winter is coming. Svetlana already had doubts about the trip just looking out the window. The wind might blow the bus off the road, she said. It would be uncomfortable walking around the village. I should go another day. This sounded ridiculous to me, but later events proved her anxiety had some basis.

I insisted, so we dressed and went out—Alla was already waiting. She pooh-poohed Svetlana's fears. It takes only forty-five minutes; Alla does it all the time.

The hour for the bus came and went. We could see the bus barn from where we stood, and the doors remained adamantly closed. We waited, debating with the other passengers what to do. At last someone went to investigate. He learned that for some unexplained reason the bus was not running that day, but another form of transport would be going—a truck taking electrical workers out to make a repair to the station in the village. There was room for a few passengers. Alla was enthusiastic and so was I, but Svetlana's complaints came faster and louder. We wouldn't be able to see out the windows. The truck might run off the road. It might not come back. I would be uncomfortable. Better to go on the bus the next time.

I reminded her of all the time we had wasted the previous year in Anadyr waiting for perfect circumstances. I would not pass up this opportunity.

At last she admitted that she was worried about her eyes. The previous year she had undergone an operation for a detached retina, and the bouncing of the truck over the bumpy dirt road was a terrifying prospect. I had forgotten about her eyes. Struck by a sudden understanding of the difference in our circumstances, I felt guilty for assuming she would come. If I had a medical problem in Providenia I could quickly fly back to a well-equipped hospital in Alaska. If something happened to her, she was in serious trouble.

Alla told Svetlana not to worry and to go home. We would be fine without her. Svetlana breathed a visible sigh of relief. With a barrage of last-minute instructions about what to say and not to say to various people, she went home, and Alla and I boarded the back of an enclosed truck. It was too noisy

The beach at New Chaplino.

to talk, and the windows were too dirty to see much, so we just hung on for the ride, which did take about forty-five minutes. I was struck that this village could be so close to the regional center and at the same time so far away, with service only once a week.

New Chaplino was built in the early 1960s on the site of a former Chukchi reindeer-herders' camp. Old Chaplino was out on a cape about forty kilometers away, and it was declared at that time to be in a strategic military zone. The entire Yupik population was moved to the new location on a protected bay that freezes in winter. This new location struck me as very beautiful, with mountains and tundra rising from the sea, but it was not advantageous for the sea-hunting Yupik people. Hunters are now far from the usual migration routes of whales, seals, and walrus and cannot keep watch for them from home. They keep their boats at another location, thirty kilometers distant. Now they cannot work or teach their children as easily as they could when their homes and hunting places were closer together.

Houses built in the 1960s were meant to be temporary but were still in use in 1994, in serious disrepair. New houses had been built recently, specially designed for hunters with places to store their boats and equipment. Predictably, these houses were taken over by members of the administration.

The village supports a fox farm where silver foxes are raised for fur hats. Food for the foxes—old walrus meat—is kept in a huge freezer. As usual, the coal burner is in the center of the village, with a mountain of coal piled outside. Since the freezers are subject to the vagaries of the electric plant, there is a powerful smell of rotting meat. I heard of another village where all the foxes died as a result of eating bad food.

We stopped at Alla's cousin's house, dropped off some groceries, and announced that we would be back for lunch. Then we were off on a whirlwind tour of Chaplino's storytellers, with brief stops in between to photograph women with facial tattoos.

There is a certain stop-start quality to doing this kind of work in Chukotka. There are long days, even weeks, when nothing happens at all, and it seems that nothing ever will. All efforts lead to nothing. Then suddenly things go into fast motion. And then stop dead again. I suspect life in the Arctic has always been like this, with busy summers and long, slow winters. I had certainly experienced it the year before, and already in a few days in Providenia there had been profound periods of inactivity.

But today Alla's pace was breathtaking. By the time we reboarded the truck at 6:30, we had recorded twelve traditional tales and some interesting information from four tellers, photographed four women with tattoos, visited the school and the community center, had lunch with Alla's cousins, and walked around the village and along the shore.

Our first stop was to see Lyuba Kutylina. She lives on the second floor in one of the larger buildings—long rows of apartments, with corridors full of fishing gear. She happened to be baby-sitting for a young grandchild who liked listening to stories as much as I did. Lyuba launched herself into old tales, moving quickly from one to another. Some were in Yupik followed by her own translation, and others were in Russian. Her voice was almost a monotone, as if she had told them many times, but not recently. She ended each story by saying, "That's all, what will I tell you next?" as if she were in a hurry to get them all out. It was only on my second visit a few weeks later that she slowed down enough for conversation.

Kivu, a Yupik woman with facial tattoos. New Chaplino.

Eagle People

There was a woman who had a child. Her husband was very bad. And the grandmother lived with them. The young wife had a hard time. Her husband beat her.

One time the grandmother took pity on her and gave her some skins. "Cook lots of food," she said. "Prepare water for yourself so you can feed yourself and your child."

"My husband will beat me again," said the girl.

"No, tomorrow he's going hunting," the grandmother replied, "and I will send you on your way."

The old woman went and took the used skins. In the old days the women used small reindeer skins instead of diapers.

The grandmother took water from washing the diapers, threw it out, and something like a big barrel appeared. She told the girl to get in.

The mother took the child, the meat, and water, and got into the barrel. The grandmother threw them into the waves.

The woman didn't know where the waves were taking them. At last she awoke and looked out through a hole. She saw that they were on a shore and the weather was quiet. She took the child out, fed him, and walked away.[1]

After a while she saw some old boards, already bleached light. "Probably there used to be a village here," she thought, and went on.

Then she saw new kindling piled up, and still she went on. Finally she came to a big yaranga. Much reindeer meat was hanging outside. She approached with the child. No one was there. She went in, cooked up some food, and ate.

After a while a man came. He was glad to see her since he didn't have a wife, and he asked her to stay. She was frightened and didn't want to live with him. But she had to stay.

At night she pinched the baby so it would cry. The man asked, "Why is the baby crying?"

"Probably he lived a long time in the tundra and doesn't want to be in the yaranga."

"Take him out in the corridor."[2]

She took the baby out in the corridor and pinched him again. The man asked again, "Why is the baby crying? Why doesn't he quiet down?"

"He lived a long time in the tundra, he doesn't like to be indoors," said the woman.

She took the baby outdoors and ran away. She came to a hill and a forest and there she saw a lake. She went up there and started to feed the baby.

Then she heard the man shouting, "Such a clever woman! When I find you I'll kill you and the baby too." He came up and looked at the lake.

She sat hiding in a tree in the forest. He saw her reflection in the lake and told her to come down.

She refused to come down.

He started to beg, and then he jumped in the air trying to get up there, still looking at the lake. She laughed softly at him. Then he came closer and she moved and fed the baby so he wouldn't cry.

"Come back and we'll go home together," he called.

She shook her head, refusing. He undressed and jumped into the lake.

When he jumped in the lake she laughed out loud. He saw her in the tree and jumped out of the water. He heard her laugh and then saw her in the tree.

He tried to get to where she was. She refused to come down.

He took up a saw and started to saw her tree down. She got away, and the tree fell right over on him and killed him.

She took the child and she walked and walked. At last she saw another yaranga. Nobody came out. She took sand and threw it onto the yaranga cover. Inside an old man said, "Daughters, go out and bring in the skins. They'll get soaked. It's raining."

The girls came out and looked around. The weather was fine. They went in and told him the weather was good.

Again the woman threw sand.

"Go look again. Maybe someone has come," said the father. One girl went out. She saw the woman and went right back in.

When she came back out she said, "The old man says if the baby is a girl, go away from here. If it is a boy, give him to me."

It was a son that she had and she gave it to the girl. The girl took the baby and went in.

The woman stood there a long time, and then she went in. Next to the old man and his daughters sat a young man. He was big and strong, with red cheeks. She said, "Where is my baby? Maybe you killed him."

The old man pointed to the young fellow and said, "This is your son."

"No," she said, "I had a baby."

"There he sits, your son," said the old man.

And the young man said, "You are my mother. Just look at my birthmark."

She realized this was her son, and she stayed there. They built their own yaranga.

It turned out these people were eagles. The girls dressed the young man in the clothes of an eagle, but at first he couldn't fly. Then he learned. He hunted and brought back whale and reindeer.

The girls said, "He is our brother."

Then when spring came the old man said, "Probably over there by Chaplino people are starting to put their boats in the water. We would like to eat fresh meat."

I think probably these eagles ate people.

They forbade the young fellow to hunt in that direction. Still, when that fellow flew off he went toward Chaplino. Many kayaks were sailing. He picked up a kayak and took some of the people home. The eagle-girls were very glad of the meat.

His mother went out and looked toward Chaplino. She saw an eagle flying and with him a kayak. The eagle-boy arrived and asked the old man which way to throw the kayak.

"That way, toward Chaplino," said the old man.

The boy threw it facing that way.

The woman looked and saw her husband, the one who was father of the child. He was lying there on the ground, dead.

"Let's cook him and eat the meat," said the eagle people. "You cook reindeer or walrus for yourself."

Probably it was that man from Chaplino that they ate. He was a bad man. A long time ago it was.

That's all![3]

The story shows the difficulties experienced by many women, the cruelty of life, and the dangers and possibilities of running away. Even when she reaches a point of personal safety, the eagle-people who take her in are cannibals—sometimes a necessity in the Arctic. The fast growth of the woman's son under the care of the eagles is a common event in folktales and recalls the spacious play of time in shamanic tradition and in the dream world. A dreamer or shaman on a journey may report events taking a very long time while only a few hours pass in this world. The time of creation is recalled in the story when the old woman throws out the water from washing the diapers and it turns into the barrel that helps the woman escape. In one myth, Raven creates the earth by defecating. In this case the baby's excrement turns into a womblike protection for him and his mother.

Lyuba told many stories that day, including one about warrior girls.[4] She also told the well-known story of Raven Koshkli, which shows another side of the ever-present raven.

The Russian folklorist E. M. Meletinskii writes about Raven's place in the epic cycles of the peoples of Siberia, Alaska, and British Columbia.[5] Raven functions on both sides of the Bering Strait as a culture hero who teaches people valuable skills, as he did in Itevtegina's story in chapter 1. Sometimes he appears as creator of heaven and earth, and sometimes as a trickster. He also shows up as the butt of others' jokes.[6] He is a shamanic mediator between heaven and earth, life and death, winter and summer. In the tale of Tsaimygyryn the shaman, which Lyuba told the same day, ravens act as shamanic helping spirits.

Meletinskii says that the peoples who live farther from the Bering Strait, such as the Tlingit and Tsimshian of British Columbia and the Koriak and Itelmen of the Kamchatka Peninsula, have continued to develop their cycles more than those such as the Chukchi, Yupik, and Northern Athabascan peoples who live between them on either side of the strait itself. As I understand Meletinskii, he postulates that those "middle" people might have moved in forming a wedge between the cultures who originated the Raven tales and who proliferated them to a greater degree. Chukchi and Yupik tales show Raven most often in his role as culture hero, whereas Koriak and Itelmen tales from Kamchatka tell of his creative powers and about his family. Trickster tales abound among the Chukchi and Yupik, as they do on the American side. As Meletinskii points out, it is also clear that raven tales form a much smaller part of the whole of Chukchi and Yupik folklore than they do on Kamchatka, where most folktales are about members of Raven's family.

Other scholars, such as Ann Chowning,[7] point out that it is unlikely that the Eskimo tales of Raven (and with them the Chukchi tales) came between the others as the result of a later migration, because those people have been in the area such a long time. She feels that the raven tales probably crossed the Bering Strait from America to Asia rather than the other way, noting that only in North America does this triple role of culture hero–transformer–dupe exist in forms other than the raven tales (as in coyote stories.)

In the Raven Koshkli tale, the shamanic aspect is introduced right away—Raven wants to sing and has no drum. In spite of this, he is the one who restores the eaglet to its family, and in doing so he is reunited with his own family. He gets the eaglet back by tricking the gray eagle—a tried and true shamanic method of soul retrieval. His tricks lend an element of humor to the serious business of bringing a soul back from the dead. Humor frequently works in Siberian shamanism to raise the energy levels of the shaman and participants in *kamlanie,* or shamanic ceremonial activities, and stories like this are one way of making people laugh.[8]

In the beliefs of many Siberian peoples, including the Yupik, the north is the direction of danger and death. This shows up clearly in Koshkli's tale. Because many rivers flow from south to north, downstream is also considered dangerous, whereas upstream, to the south, is beneficial. Conflict between ravens and eagles is characteristic of raven lore. Another common theme is the woman as mediator—in this case the brother-eagle's wife convinces him not to kill the baby ravens. Often women storytellers include this kind of minor character; men may leave them out. The woman's telling emphasizes the importance of the wisdom and clairvoyant ability of female members of society.

Raven Koshkli

Raven Koshkli lived with his wife. He wanted to sing a song but had no drum. He said to his wife, "Go to my brother and tell him I want to sing a song." That's his brother crow.

His wife flew and flew and met bad weather. Suddenly she stopped. She looked around and there was an eagle. He grabbed her and wanted to take her home so she would be his wife. And so she stayed there with him.

Koshkli waited for his wife. He waited and waited, and finally couldn't wait any more. And the wife started to grind her teeth.

Eagle said, "Why are you grinding your teeth? You have everything here, you have meat. Eat."

She said, "I don't have everything. I'm lonely because at home I have two sons."

"Ah yes, two sons. Never mind, tomorrow I'll go get them."

Next day the eagle flew off to get the two babies and brought them back. He had a son, too, and told the baby ravens to fly with the eagle. At first the raven babies couldn't keep up and fell to the ground from tiredness. But then they started to fly fast, faster than the eagle himself.

The big eagle said, "Never fly in the northern direction, it's dangerous there."

The three flew together, and one day the small eagle said to the ravens, "Let's fly that way, to the north."

"Your father said not to fly that way," said the ravens. "It's dangerous."

"Well, if we see something dangerous, we'll fly away."

They flew away to the north, and then a gray eagle came toward them. He grabbed the eaglet and took him home. The ravens flew back. The eaglet's father started to ask them questions.

"Why did you leave him?"

"We were forbidden to go that way but eaglet said if there was something scary we would come back. We left him when the gray eagle caught him."

"That gray eagle is nasty, he took my son. Tomorrow you will fly to the south. My brother lives there. Call him so he will help me."

The baby ravens flew and flew and at last came to the place where the brother lived. When they arrived, the brother's wife was there alone.

"Eat quickly and hide," she said. "When he comes back, he will kill you." The wife told them to hide and they did.

Then the big eagle's brother flew up and circled around saying, "I smell something, somebody must be here. Who is here? I'll kill them!"

"Why kill?" said his wife. "Your brother sent them to you for help because the gray eagle took away the one who is like your own son to you."

The ravens came out of their hiding place. Then the three flew back to the eagle.

"It's going to be hard to get that gray eagle. He's very strong. Let's call Koshkli. He's clever," said the big eagle. That's the one whose wife he had stolen!

He flew to Koshkli himself. "Gray eagle took my son," he said. "Koshkli, you are clever. Help me."

And so the two went home to the eagle's place and there Koshkli saw his wife. Eagle slept with his own wife. The next day all five set off, the two small ravens, the two eagles, and Koshkli.

Raven Koshkli hid the others. He went on and met the one who had been taken. He met the young eagle who had been stolen. The eaglet said, "Why have you come?"

"Your friends are hidden in the hills. Tomorrow, refuse to go hunting and we will run off with you."

Then Koshkli started to eat some very old whale meat where the gray eagle could see him.

The eaglet came down and started to talk with the gray eagle.

"What does Koshkli want?" said gray eagle. "Clever one, where has he come from? Here he is eating that old whale meat. What is he trying to think up?"

They called Koshkli over. "What do you want? You're probably up to some clever business as usual."

"No," he said, "I just came here to eat. We have nothing to eat at home. You have an excellent son," he said, praising the young eagle.

"Yes, a fine son. He brings me reindeer and whales." Gray eagle calmed down. He went on praising the son, saying, "He's strong!"

"I would never leave this village," Koshkli said.

Next day they woke up, and gray eagle got ready to fly away to catch a moose. He asked the son, "Aren't you going anywhere today?"

"No, I have no bullets, I'll stay here and make some."

Gray eagle flew away and Koshkli said to the eaglet, "Let's fly away. Your father is there and your brothers and uncle."

They got ready to go, and just after they started out, gray eagle came back.

"You're so clever," he called, "I will tear you apart."

The eaglet was flying away with Koshkli's sons.

They looked back and saw gray eagle's mouth wide open with his tongue hanging out from tiredness. Gray eagle circled. He wouldn't let himself be caught.

The sons were not sorry for him and attacked him. They tore him apart and dropped the pieces on the ground. The three flew on until they came to the white eagle's house.

"Where is the gray eagle?" asked the white eagle.

"We killed the gray eagle."

When Koshkli finally arrived, he fell asleep exhausted with his wife and sons.

That's all![9]

Next Lyuba told the tale of a human shaman, Tsaimygyryn, and his raven helpers. In the first part of the story we see how the shaman gains more power after he marries two wives whom he steals from other men. His singing gets stronger, and at last he is ready to heal the sick. It is amusing that the spirit helpers tell the shaman how much the family should pay for the healing.

Clothing is also crucial here. At first the shaman has no clothes and cannot travel in winter. Then he puts on bird clothing in order to fly, in the same way the boy did in "The Eagle People," and he asks for the clothing of the sick boy, which helps to find him. As in most Siberian cultures, shapechanging is seen by the Yupik as a change of clothes.[10]

Tsaimygyryn the Shaman

There lived a shaman called Tsaimygyryn. He had no wife. He had sores all over his body. He sang songs every day. And then the spirit-raven knocked. Tsaimygyryn said, "Come in." The spirit told him, "In the tundra there is a man who has a second wife. Go and get her."

"How will I go to the tundra with no clothes? I'll freeze."

"What? Do you refuse to go when I tell you?"

"I'll go tomorrow," said Tsaimygyryn.

In the morning he set out. He came to a hill, and a door opened. A man was calling to him, "Come here." He came to the man, and there was a woman there too. They fed him well.

The man said, "When I was young, your father left us five dogs. Take them and go on your way. You'll go slowly. But take this rope too. Then you'll go fast." In the morning he got ready. The man brought out five ravens—they were the sled dogs. Tsaimygyryn put them on and flew away.

He came to the last yaranga. A woman came out. "Why did you come here?" she asked.

"I came here to take the cannibal's second wife."

"Don't talk like that. He'll hear you." She gave him some food. He started to eat and the spirit knocked. "Why are you eating alone, without feeding me?" it said.

Tsaimygyryn told the woman to go out and look. She went out and looked all around. No one was there, just one raven cawing. She came back and told him, "There's nothing but one raven."

"Go and tell that raven that Tsaimygyryn will eat with him."

She went out and called. The raven jumped and jumped, and came in and ate with him.

Then a young woman looked in through the opening and said, "The boss says to go home. Why should I marry you? You're too dirty and sick, covered with scabs." She went away, and then she came back. "The boss says to go home," she said again. Tsaimygyryn got sick of this—he threw her to the ground and she stuck there. He embraced her and kissed her.

The boss was thinking, "Why hasn't she come back? Go and find out." He sent some fellows to find out. They looked and saw Tsaimygyryn lying with the woman. They came back and told the boss, "Your wife is lying with Tsaimygyryn, and he is kissing her."

"Give me my spear," said the husband.

He took his spear and went and looked in. There lay Tsaimygyryn, probably kissing her. The husband was about to approach—when he got stuck to the floor!

"Will I always stay like this, stuck to the floor?" he asked Tsaimygyryn.

"Yes, you will. Soon you'll die of hunger. And I'll take all your things."

"What do you want?"

"I want your wife, and also those skins and bags."

"You can have them. Just let me go."

So the shaman let him go. The man went off, and his wife too.

Next morning the wife knocked and said, "Let's go home quickly. And bring that bag of skins." She was afraid. They went home.

And now that he had that wife, he began to sing more than before.

Again the spirit-raven knocked. "Tsaimygyryn, go to the north. A man lives there with two wives. Take away the second wife."

"All right, I'll go tomorrow."

Next day he took the five ravens and put them on. When he got there a woman came out and said, "Why have you come?"

"I've come to take one of the boss's wives."

Then the young woman came and said, "You are too dirty, you have too many scabs and sores."

He lay her down.

Again the boss said, "Where is my wife?" and sent someone to find out. The fellows went and saw her with Tsaimygyryn and went back and told.

"Give me my spear," said the husband. "I'll kill him."

And like the first one, he, too, got stuck to the floor.

"Tsaimygyryn, will I stay like this forever?"

"Yes, you will. You'll die and I'll take all your things."

"What do you want?"

"I want your wife and five bags of fox and other skins."

"Take them. Just let me go."

So Tsaimygyryn let him go. Next day the woman said, "Let's go home."

They went home, and now he had two wives. He sang even stronger than before.

The spirit-raven knocked again.

"Tsaimygyryn, go to the tundra," it said. "There the only son of a reindeer herder is dying. Go and bring him to life."

Next day he put on the ravens and left. He came to the herder's camp. "Our son is very sick," they said. "Go to the yaranga at the back. A woman is there, our relative. If our son were not sick we wouldn't do this. I would not tell you to leave."

He found the woman, and she gave him something to eat. Again that raven knocked. "Are you going to eat alone, without feeding me?"

He told the woman to go out. She went out and saw the raven. There is just the one raven, waiting. She said to the raven, "Tsaimygyryn says he will not eat alone."

The raven came in and ate. Everyone was crying. The reindeer herder came in and he was crying, too. "Our only son has died." And the woman told him, "This Tsaimygyryn arrived. He is probably a shaman. While he was eating a raven knocked, and he told me to go out. I went and nobody was there, just the raven. He said to call the raven and now they are eating together."

The mother asked Tsaimygyryn, "Did my son really die? Come and look and tell me before it is too late. Is he really dead?"

"Give me clothes and I'll go."

They gave him the boy's clothes. He got to where the boy was and said, "Why are you crying? If I am not successful, then you can cry." Suddenly the spirit knocked, with all the family sitting there.

"If they say they'll give you half the herd," said the spirit, "then bring him back. If they don't agree, don't bring him."

"Just bring him back," said the herdsman.

"When he was small," said the shaman, "didn't he kill anything? Do you have anything left?"

"Only this bird skin."

"Give it to me so that I can put it on."

They moistened it thoroughly and stretched it. He put it on and flew away. He saw two eagles sitting and asked them for clothes. They agreed and gave him eagle clothes. He turned into an eagle. He flew and flew and came to a yaranga. He looked in through a hole. There a woman was washing the floor. The soul of the boy who had died was in a basin, and there were baskets all around. Tsaimygyryn came in and chased the woman. She went out. He took the boy's soul and flew away. The small woman came back and said, "What kind of a bird was that?" as if he had offended her. She looked and the basin was empty.

She started chasing him, but he got back to where the eagles were sitting. He succeeded in getting dressed as an eagle again and flew away. The woman didn't catch him.

He brought the boy back to life. They had promised half a herd of reindeer. He brought the boy to life and they gave him the reindeer. Tsaimygyryn took five plants, threw them out, and they turned into five little people. He told them to take the reindeer back to his home on the shore. Tsaimygyryn quickly went home. He had those five ravens and he flew quickly.

Beside him there lived a big spirit, and she had a grandson. When there was a big blizzard he took down those five plants. That grandmother was envious and said, "You are lucky. What are you eating—fresh reindeer meat?" They were cooking. They ate and drank bouillon. Meanwhile the grandmother shouted at the reindeer and they turned into gulls. Many of them flew over the sea.

Tsaimygyryn said to his wife, "How did I offend that grandmother? Now all my reindeer have turned into gulls. I have no herd. Why did I offend her?"

He dressed for the storm and went over there. He gathered those plants and took them. "I'm sorry for you," he said. "Where is your grandson?"

"At home."

"Alone?"

"Alone."

"Let me go and look after him." Tsaimygyryn went and he killed the grandson. He cut him up into little pieces. He took the cutting board and mixed the pieces together. Tsaimygyryn shouted at the pieces and they turned into ducks. They flew away to the shore.

Tfai! I'm done!

Apparently the plants in this story have power of transformation. I suspect that this grandmother at the end of the story is another shaman with whom Tsaimygyryn is in competition, and this is why he refused her food and killed her grandson. This ultimate proof of his great power lends clarity to an otherwise abrupt ending.

Weeks later I came back to Chaplino alone on the bus. That day, without Alla, I moved more slowly. I visited Lyuba, and she told me a lot more about shamans, healing, and the mixture of old Yupik beliefs with Christianity. Often today Yupik visitors come from Alaska and tell their Asian relatives about their Christian beliefs and practices. "Before they eat, they talk with God," says Lyuba. "We don't do that, but we make offerings when we go out."

It often happens when I ask about shamans that a person will say there were none and then promptly go on to tell about a healing. Elderly women in both Tuva and the Amur region have approached telling about their own experience of shamanic healing by first saying that they had no memories about shamans.

"I didn't see shamans myself," said Lyuba, "but they used to sing strongly. And those spirits would really knock strongly. When the shaman started to sing he told me to lie down, and he himself sat. This is when I was a little girl. They all sang together strongly, a whole group. And the spirit knocked strongly, strongly. And it came right from behind me. And jumped, as if it was really big, when in fact it was small.

"I was just a little girl. I didn't believe at first that there was a God. At first it felt like these little steps walking on my body, from around the left side. And a sound, as if it were really big. It came up and started a conversation with me.

"I was sick and got better. Many times I almost died: I was very, very sick. When they tell about God, I believe that it is probably true. Because when I was very sick as a girl, I woke up so thin, as if in a dream. I saw a white man and they said that I had gone up there above. And I sort of got better.

"I started to listen about the Russian God, or what the American Yupik said. Probably that one helped me. Also when I was coughing blood. I used to suffer from tuberculosis but now they have taken it away. They took me to the hospital in bad condition. Probably I was starting to die. And in my dream I saw a man in white clothes. He told me to stand up."

The man in white clothes recalls both the Christian God and the traditional funeral clothing of the Yupik, which was white. It is clear that Lyuba's idea about the Christian God is not one of exclusivity. He takes his place alongside the other gods who receive her respect.

"I got up then. I think it was God who helped me. I started to get up and it was as if I couldn't move. And he poured medicine right onto me, the pills that the doctors gave us. That man in white poured those pills on me and I started to get better.

"When I sit and think, I think it was probably God who helped me. I was dying but someone helped. Now when I start to get a little sick, I go up there on the hill. He says come right up. When I get up there I start to get better. God helped. When we see something, when we go out we always offer something, we feed the spirits."

One way in which traditional Yupik beliefs differ from the Christian is in the importance of the spirits of place, which are central to Siberian philosophy. These spirits receive offerings and blessings from people and are helpful if treated well. But they can also affect a person in a dangerous way, especially in the tundra and beside the sea, where it is easy to get lost and where death can overtake a person in a moment. Stories like Lyuba's show what happens when a person does not treat the spirits of place the way they should.

She says that when you are walking in the tundra you might see a crack in the earth. "You might see something open up in the earth. You look and it's all dark in that direction. If you see something tempting—a good village with warm houses and people beckoning to you—don't go down there. If somebody you are with wants to go, hit him. If you feel strongly tempted, breaking your own nose is a good way to come to your senses. Pissing on the crack will also close it up.

"One woman came very close to losing her mind and going down there.

They were calling her, saying, 'Come down here.' She was about to put her foot in the crack, but her dog pulled her back.

"People used to get lost before. When we lived at Sigluk one Chukchi got lost. His brothers looked and looked for him but couldn't find him. They said he was wearing snowshoes. They followed his tracks, and it looked as if he had taken one last step and then was lost. He disappeared completely, right there on the road where people went by from Chaplino and Yanrekinot.

"And at Yanrekinot it happened—that fellow disappeared! Then a sleigh came from Nunligran—that's a long way from us. They came and stopped. They said one herder, a shaman, was out walking. He turned, and behind him saw a man flying! Just like that, a man was flying. The shaman had a rope with him for lassoing reindeer—he took the rope and lassoed the man. The man fell.

"The shaman roped him in and then questioned him. 'Where are you from?'

"'Yanrekinot,' the man replied.

"And so they sent two sleighs from Nunligran. I was just a little girl then. They came and asked about him.

"His brothers went to Nunligran and got him. And it was the one who had got lost. Just last year he died, that man.

"So you see he had flown all the way from Yanrekinot to Nunligran, and if that shaman had not caught him he probably would have flown further.

"He died not long ago. I just don't remember who it was. I was little at the time. The older people used to tell us about things like that so we would be sure to feed the spirits. They told us and we listened."[11]

At certain points in physical or spiritual geography, a person can enter another reality. This is probably what happens in the following story to a man who gets lost in the fog. He stumbles across some whale hunters, and when he arrives home with them he becomes a type of supernatural being with powers of bringing illness and healing. His story is unique in being told from his own point of view.

On the other hand, it is possible that the man dies while lost in the fog and that this is why people cannot see or hear him when he comes near them. It is widely believed that the souls of people who have died without proper funerals can cause problems for the living, although usually they tend to stay around their own families. In this story the man shows up around unfamiliar people.

The girl's illness in the story sounds like tuberculosis, because it is transmitted by coughing and comes into the community through contact with the outside world.

The Man Who Got Lost in the Fog

A man was hunting and got lost in the fog. He sailed on and then saw a place where people had killed a whale. There were many boats. He approached and spoke, but nobody answered. He cut off a piece of meat and ate with them, and together with them he tied the whale to a boat.

He went with them. He talked but still no one answered.

They came to a village. There were lots of people on shore. And as they used to do when the first whale was killed, people came out dancing.

A girl came out all undressed carrying a container for hiding meat.[12] The man came onto the shore and again tried to talk to the people there. No one answered. They cut off pieces of skin and meat and everybody ate. He ate a piece, and some skin got caught in his throat. He coughed, and the piece flew out and stuck onto that girl's back, onto her shoulder blade. She began to get very sick. She even fell down from the sickness. They picked her up and saw that whale skin on her back.

She was the daughter of the boss. People came to try to bring her to life. The man came too, but nobody talked to him. Nobody saw him.

A woman went into a yaranga and came back. "He'll be right here," she said.

It was full moon weather. A man came from a yaranga carrying a drum and some other things. That shaman stood beside the man. The shaman said, "Oh, what a full moon."

The man said, "Yes, yesterday it was less but today it is full."

So the shaman asked, "So you speak our language?"

"Yes."

"Where are you from?"

"I got lost in the fog and saw the boats where they had killed a whale. I tried to talk but no one answered. No one saw me. I came here with them.

That girl has whale skin stuck to her that came from me when I coughed—it's stuck to her shoulder blade. That's why she is sick."

The shaman said, "When it gets dark I will sing. I'll tell them to bring her to me, and you take the whale skin off with your hands."

Again the man approached, but no one saw him or talked to him. The shaman told him to sit next to him. He sat there and ate. The girl was in a very serious condition. The man saw the whale skin and took it off a little way.

The shaman said to the people, "It's getting dark. I'll sing. Bring her to me." So they brought her to the shaman. "Take that skin off her. But first I'll tell you this. A man came here with you. When you killed the whale a man came in a boat and then came here. You can see him after my song."

"No," said the people, "we don't want to see him."

The girl got even sicker. The shaman said, "Take off that skin." The man took off some more, and she got even worse. He began to touch her with his hands. Then she breathed better.

Again people said, "No, we don't want to see him. Let your spirit helper take him away."

"You will see him," said the shaman. "He came with you."

The girl began to breathe well. It got light and they saw the man. They began to see the man who had come with them and asked, "Where did you come from?"

He said, "I was hunting and got lost in the fog and saw where you had killed the whale. I came with you and talked and talked but no one answered or saw me. I ate with you on shore and coughed and that thin whale skin landed on her shoulder blade and stuck there. She got sick."

As soon as he said this and it got light—he disappeared. When the weather got better he went away from there.

Lyuba told me one last tale. The theme of the despised orphan is repeated over and over again in the folklore of the north.[13] It is the duty of the uncle to take good care of his brother's child, but clearly this is not always done. The orphan often receives supernatural aid. Here it comes from a man in the corridor of the subterranean house—that zone between the inside and the outside, the natural and the supernatural.

The Orphan with Sharp Hands

There was an orphan. He didn't have anybody, no parents, no brothers or sisters. He lived with an uncle. When they were at home the uncle didn't give him anything to eat. When the uncle went hunting, his wife would give the boy a little bit to eat. And when he came back the uncle would say, "You must be feeding him, that's why he's not getting skinny."

And she would say, "Why should I feed him when his own relative won't? I don't want to feed him." And when they had finished eating the uncle would throw him leftovers from the big tough pieces of walrus meat. All night the boy chewed and chewed.

Then from the corridor the boy heard someone bump his head. The boy looked—in those days there were no doors, just reindeer skins hanging.

The boy looked. A man was standing there.

"What's the matter? Is your uncle not feeding you?" asked the man.

"He just gives me these tough pieces and I can't chew them." He showed the man a piece of meat.

And that man said, "I'll show you what to do." He blew on his hand and then used it to cut the meat so the boy could eat it.

"You, too, blow on your hand and then you'll be able to cut the meat," he said.

The boy blew on his hand. He cut the meat and ate.

"Tomorrow do that same thing," said the man, "and you'll always be able to eat."

The man in the corridor disappeared.

The boy went to sleep feeling very satisfied. In the morning he woke up afraid of his uncle who yelled at him. Whenever the uncle went hunting the woman would give the boy something to eat. This time she brought in some frozen walrus meat and she couldn't cut it.

"Let me cut it," said the boy.

"You're so thin," she answered, "how will you cut walrus meat?"

But the boy said, "Let me try."

The boy blew on his palm and then started to cut the meat. The woman said, "Quick, take a piece for yourself."

He began to eat. The woman took the frozen meat that the boy had cut and put it in the corridor.

The uncle came back and set out the special cutting board, *ayut'ka,* and began to cut meat.

He said to his wife, "You should have brought this in sooner. How are you going to cut this frozen meat?"

The woman turned to the boy and said, "You cut it," and the man said, "How will he cut it, he's so skinny?"

All the same, the boy blew on his hand. Holding it a distance above, he cut the meat into small pieces.

After this he started to eat with them. The man said, "Eat with us," and the boy started to eat with them.

The man said to his wife, "Tomorrow I won't go hunting. When I go out, I'll see somebody and I'll ask them to come in and eat. You'll bring out the frozen meat."

He started to respect that boy. He saw him cut the meat. The next day the uncle didn't go hunting. He went outside and looked around. He saw somebody and said to him, "Come to us and eat."

They came in and he said to his wife, "A guest has come, let's eat."

The woman set out the board and brought in some frozen meat. The man who had come to visit said, "Why did you bring that?"

They called the boy.

"How can he cut the meat, he's so skinny?" said the guest.

The uncle sat down. He was in a good mood. The boy blew on his hand and started to cut the frozen walrus meat from above. He cut it thin as thin.

The uncle said, "You eat with us, too."

After that the boy ate with them, and he started to live well. Probably that uncle was afraid the boy would blow on his hand one day and kill him!

That's all!

6 / Chaplino II

Killer whales can help people. When they see a sinking *baidara*
[walrus-skin boat] they can take it up, two of them, and bring it
to shore. I've seen it happen. And our people have only to give
them a piece of tobacco if they have some, or a bit of cigarette if
they have none. In thanks. The whales are very close to people.

—Gleb Nakazik

During my first trip to Chaplino, when I rode on that bouncing truck with
Alla Panaug'ye, we visited the Chaplino school, which was not in session.
Some of the teachers were there, however, and I was introduced to Alla's
school friends who have come back to their community to teach. This is the
generation that has been away to study in regional centers and sometimes in
Moscow and St. Petersburg. Like Viktor Tymnev'ye, Valentina Rintuv'ye, and
Svetlana Chuklinova, they value the culture of their ancestors and feel the
need for the new generation of children to know their heritage.

One of the teachers at Chaplino school was Nina Trapeznikova. She was
teaching art in grades five through eleven, especially to the girls. Her students produced high-quality beadwork, drawings, and fur mosaics. They
were getting some materials from Alaska, but there was still a severe short-
age. Her classroom, even without students in session, was warm and full of
life, in contrast to the cold wind, ramshackle houses, and coal smoke outdoors in the village.

Nina said she told the children stories that she heard from her own parents. She tells the stories in Russian, and they are well worked out. This is the

one she told me, surrounded by empty seats and the art projects of Chaplino's children.

Yumima

There was a girl called Yumima. She was an orphan, and when she grew up she got married. Her husband was a hunter. When he was away she stayed home and cooked. There used to be these oil lamps. They cooked food, they dried meat and clothes on the lamp. They also cooked on a fire in the yaranga. You always had to look after the lamp and make sure it didn't go out. When her husband came back from the hunt, she had to dry his clothes, cook on the lamp, boil meat, feed him, and keep things warm and light. She took good care of her *achak*-lamp.

Yumima's husband came back from the hunt. He was not an ordinary person, he was a devil. This is a story, after all! He came and called, "Yumima!" She came running. "Beat out my clothes." In the old days they used to beat the clothes with a special stick, a beater made of reindeer antler. When the clothes got full of snow they beat them. He had a fur parka, pants of sealskin, seal boots, and warm socks inside.

Yumima beat the snow and he yelled at her, "You're too slow!" and he took the stick and started to beat her. And thus she suffered, Yumima. She did everything fast and yet to him it seemed that she was slow.

Once when he was hunting she went outside for a little walk and the lamp went out. She came back, and when she saw the lamp she started to feel afraid. She was afraid her husband would come and there she would be with nothing cooked, everything cold and dark. She worried. Where would she get fire? There were no dwellings nearby.

She took the lamp and went off, not caring which way she walked. She didn't get far from home before she saw a big house, a yaranga. She came up to the entrance and called, "Who's there?"

Nobody answered.

She looked inside. It was light there, and so warm! The yaranga was clean and beautiful inside. In the corner a lamp was burning. Instead of fire there were many different beautiful beads burning. Just flowing over. Yumima came up to the lamp, looking at it. And then she heard footsteps—

someone was coming. Quickly she took one bead, put it in her mouth, and kept it behind her cheek.

She hid. There was a big container there, for food, and she hid behind that. The woman of the house came in. She looked and saw that the lamp was flickering—one bead was missing. The woman asked, "What's the matter with you, lamp?" The lamp kept flickering and flickering.

"Where is the bead?"

The lamp answered, "Yumima, Yumima."

"Where is Yumima?"

"Behind the container, behind the container." The woman came over, picked it up, and there was Yumima. In her cheek was a bead.

"Yumima, give me the bead."

Yumima gave her the bead, she put it back in place, and the lamp started to burn clearly. All the colors of the rainbow in that beautiful lamp.

Then the woman said, "Yumima, I know you well."

You see, this was a kind magician.

"I appeared to you specially, with my house," she said. "Your husband is a devil. I want to help. I will teach you how to live, and you will not know grief. I know, you don't have to tell me what happened. Your lamp went out and you were left without fire. I will give you fire.

"Don't be afraid. Go home and all will be well. When your husband tries to rush you, don't hurry, just do things gradually. If he sends you for stroganina (they make stroganina by freezing fish or meat and shaving it and eating it with salt), you always run, but he thinks you're slow and begins to beat you. Don't rush, just go outside, stand there a bit, and then go in. If you do everything slowly, without rushing, your husband will praise you."

And so the woman gave Yumima fire, and she went home and lit her lamp.

Her husband comes—he calls, "Yumima, beat out the snow." She goes out to him and unhurriedly begins to beat out the snow.

He says, "This is the way it should be."

He says "Go get stroganina."

She doesn't rush but goes outside and stands there a bit, breathing the fresh air, and then goes in. And he is so happy. At last, this is the way it should be.

And from that time Yumima started to live well.

That's all!

As a teacher Nina adds detail about how people used to live. This was for my benefit and that of modern children who may never have seen a *yaranga*. It is interesting that she makes the bad husband a devil, whereas in Lyuba's stories and in Bogoras's there are bad husbands who beat their wives without being devils. Some storytellers make very bad behavior into something truly inhuman, in the form of a devil or an evil spirit, perhaps to distance it from acceptable human behavior. Others tellers describe things simply as they happened.

There are many familiar themes in the story, including the helpful old woman and the importance of fire. Nina emphasizes the beauty of fire as well as its usefulness. Bogoras wrote, "The lamp and everything with it are considered a highly efficient protection against spirits."[1]

Nina's story is original in its image of the beads in the lamp. Nor have I heard anywhere else about the value of not rushing. This seems to be a rather contemporary value. But life in Chukotka has always been full of contrast between moving fast during the endless days of summer and enjoying plenty of time during the endless nights of winter. In the realm of vision created by story and trance, time disappears. Yumima makes a visit to that world where time is a matter of perception and vision, and she is able to bring that gift back to this world in order to calm her husband's ill temper. Nina's description of the sense of having plenty of time and the comfort it creates is especially valuable in the modern world.

Throughout my busy day in Chaplino on that first visit, Alla had left me alone with storytellers to go about her own business, reappearing in time to take me to the next place. Outdoors we stopped to photograph elderly women with facial tattoos who were sitting in the weak fall sunlight. All day Alla was trying to call one last storyteller, with no success.

Finally she said, "We'll just have to go looking for him. You should hear Nakazik. He is our best storyteller and really knows Yupik folklore. He worked with Menovshchikov on his editions."

We came to a house at the far end of the village. Nobody answered when Alla knocked, so we went in. Beyond the entrance hallway, full of boots and fishing gear, was a corridor with several doors opening from it, all closed.

This is an *obshchezhitie,* a type of communal apartment common to older construction in Russia, designed so that several people or sometimes families share one communal kitchen and bath.[2]

Alla found her way to the kitchen, where people were drinking tea, and asked which door to knock on.

"Gleb Alexandrovich!" she called. "Can we come in?" At the same time she turned the doorknob. This seems to be a typical approach in Russia. By traditional custom, a guest simply enters and waits at the door to be acknowledged.

We came into a small room containing a metal-frame bed, a couple of straight chairs, and a table covered with photographic equipment that looked to me as if it should be called historic.

On the bed lay a man with a book across his stomach and the disheveled look of a person caught napping. He sat up hastily, checking his clothing. His hair was sticking out in all directions.

"Gleb Alexandrovich," said Alla, "this is Kira. She's come from Canada and she wants to hear old stories." The twinkle in her eye grew more intense. "We've heard that you are the best storyteller around. Won't you tell her something?"

He moved over and patted the bed beside him. "It happened a long time ago . . ." he said. This was a storyteller who wasted no time! I stopped him long enough to get out the tape recorder.

"She has an hour and then we have to catch our ride to Providenia," said Alla. "I'll be back." And off she went.

"So you want to hear old stories, do you?" said Nakazik. "What for?"

"I tell stories myself, in Canada. I'd like to learn some Yupik stories to tell, so people there will get to know more about you. And I would like to publish them in English."

"All right. I'll tell you one of our clan legends. They say that when much time goes by, events from life turn into real tales."

The Girl Who Wintered in the Graveyard

In our clan, Lyakavut, one girl refused to marry. This was in old Chaplino. One night when it got dark she went out of the village in the direction away from the cape and farther along. In that direction was the graveyard.

There between the village and the cemetery she stopped and sat with her legs bent up in front of her face. She covered her head with her hood and cried. She didn't want to marry.

She heard steps crunching along the stones. Someone came up to her and said, "Come with me." It was dark and raining. She followed this woman—it *was* a woman. They walked in the direction of the cemetery, and as they got closer they saw someone's house there, a type of yaranga. It belonged to one of the clan ancestors, beside her grave. That girl started to speak to the woman and stayed there to live.

When it was time to lie down and go to sleep the woman urged her strongly to lie with her feet not that way, but with her head this way. And so it was.

Much time went by—in short, she spent the whole winter there with that woman.

One night this woman woke the girl up. "Go out and look," she said. Outside the opening the girl saw an old woman, a black sorcerer. There was such a person who did bad deeds from Chaplino. The old woman closed all the tapes on her hood and did her black deeds there in the cemetery.

"I'll go look," thought the girl. She came up to that sorcerer, touched her, and saw her face. The woman was so frightened!

"Don't tell anyone that you saw me," said the girl.

"In Chaplino they thought that you got lost."

"I didn't expect to see you either, but I won't tell."

They agreed that neither would tell. And literally in a couple of days that old woman died and they buried her. She hadn't survived the fright.

And so they lived, the girl and her ancestor.

Again another time the woman woke the girl up and she looked out and saw a huge dog, securely tied. All covered in blood. In our belief people have an aura, or double. This double was all bloody. And as it happened, in the village one day later another person was buried.

When spring came that woman said, "Enough, go home. Your mother is waiting for you, and your father thinks you have died. Enough of this, it's time for you to start a family." She talked to the girl, saying that in order to carry on your clan you must get married.

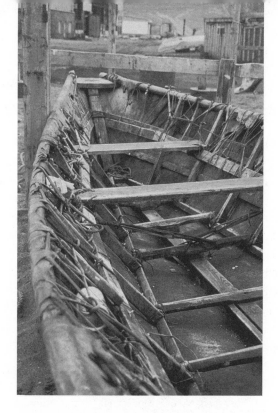

A walrus-skin baidara. Sireniki.

"Go home. The hunters have already gone on the first spring hunt, out in baidaras for walrus. Just one thing—when you get home you'll find there is terrible hunger in Chaplino. You may eat even very old meat—any kind of meat, just don't eat of the plants."

"But if I go I'll frighten them."

"Right. Don't go straight to your own yaranga, first go to one of the neighbor's."

And so the girl went to one of the neighboring yarangas. "Go tell my mother that I'm alive," she told them. "I've come from far away."

"Maybe they've stopped believing you'll come back. They think maybe you froze or something," said the neighbor.

All the same, it sometimes happens that someone comes back even after a very long time. So the mother had prepared; she guessed that the girl was alive.

"Yes, she is alive," said the neighbor and told all.

The girl came home and the mother was overjoyed. She cried and embraced her. The girl told everything, how she had spent the winter with their dead ancestor. And then the daughter said, "Oh, how I want to eat. I'm so hungry."

"We have nothing," said the mother, "the stores are empty. The hunters just went out."

The girl looked outside and saw that very plant that the woman had forbidden her to eat. She took just two fingers of that plant to her mouth and suddenly from everywhere, from her mouth, eyes, nostrils, came that same plant in a huge quantity.

She died. After spending the whole winter with that woman.

People knew that she had come back. They started to come to the house. But then they heard a terrible cry from the mother.

"My daughter died!" the mother cried through all Chaplino.

The hunters came back. The hunt was successful and the girl's father thought, "Why hasn't my wife come out to meet me, even though we've killed walrus?"

Everyone hid from his eyes, nobody wanted to give him the bad news.

"Is my wife alive?" he asked. No one replied. He tried to guess, thinking, "What happened?"

Again he heard that same strong loud cry. He went home to his wife and she told him what had happened. "Just as soon as we saw our daughter! Now we have to bury her."

That's one of the things they tell in our clan legends.

I wish I had asked him what it meant. Was the girl already dead because of spending the winter in the graveyard? Was the plant poisonous? If so, why did so much of it come out of her body? Perhaps the plant was normally edible and the girl's death provided a great quantity for people to eat. Or the story might explain why a certain plant that grows in great quantity may not be eaten. It could be like the plants used by the shaman Tsaimygyryn in transformation, gone wrong this time. In light of Lyuba's tales in which people appear in other realities, it is possible that this girl appears to her family after her own death in the same way that the doubles appeared to her in the graveyard. Forgetting what one has learned in the realm of spirit or dream is a popular folklore theme the world over.

The theme of the girl who refuses to marry is quite common, and the outcomes vary considerably. In some cases the girl marries a whale or walrus;[3] in others she regrets her rebellion and comes home. In one tale from the Menovshchikov collection, the girl creates sea creatures and tundra people from small objects she takes from home.[4] Just as a woman's marriage with a whale explores the ambiguous relationship of reverence for a food animal, perhaps this story explores some of the same issues in terms of plants.

The girl's refusal to marry is far from being a refusal to procreate. In Arctic society there was considerable sexual freedom, and the girl's being unmarried does not imply that she is not sexual. Instead, her refusal has social implications about marriage as a contract between families, where procreation is specifically meant to carry on a family or clan lineage. It speaks also about times when a socially appropriate husband cannot be found and a woman carries on the family without marriage. Refusal to marry is a creative act, and Menovshchikov believes it goes back to a time when female deities were more revered than they are now.[5]

Because people's doubles routinely appear at the cemetery before death, perhaps the story speaks of a girl's undergoing a long illness, almost recovering, and finally dying. Her time in the graveyard might have led to a shamanic death and rebirth, since she deals successfully with the black sorcerer.[6] But she still dies because of eating the forbidden plant. On the other hand, shamanic initiation is often successful precisely because a person does what is forbidden. The tale is a mystery.

The next story Gleb Nakazik told was more humorous than tragic. It was like one that Margarita Takakava had told the year before.[7]

Reindeer, Crow, and Evil Spirit

There was a herder who had only a few reindeer. An evil spirit kept coming around chasing those reindeer off in all directions.

The crow decided to help the herdsman.

The evil spirit wanted to fly, and the crow agreed to help him if he wouldn't bother those reindeer any more.

The evil spirit got up on the back of the crow's neck. Up they went until the earth looked the size of a sealskin.

They went further, until the earth looked the size of a dish, and still further, until the whole earth looked the size of the heel part of a boot sole.

Then the crow turned over and dropped the evil spirit.

Now he was flying! When he flew right side up he laughed, "Ho, ho, ho!" When he flew upside down he pulled in his breath, "Ahhhh!"

Over and over he went until he landed back on the earth. He landed headfirst and sank into the ground so that only his legs were sticking up.

The herder came back from gathering up his reindeer, and he was delighted. At last he had a place to tie them to!

I asked if some evil spirits had one eye, and Nakazik said yes, they have different looks, and some have one eye. But he didn't tell a story about one. He seemed a bit disappointed that he had told a story I had already heard from someone else, and went on.

Scraping the Sky

Stop me if you know this one.

Five brothers went hunting in the wintertime, and they got caught by a storm, a terrible storm. The eldest says, "Let's all take hands and just walk along opposite the wind." So they walked and walked and suddenly came up against something.

Yaranga! They went in and it was warm and light inside, so nice! Several lamps were burning.

"Guests have come to me," said a woman, turning to meet them. She dried their clothes and fed them. She hung their boots up and repaired their pants. Then she said, "I'm going out. No matter what happens, don't you go out. Don't even look outdoors."

All right, the brothers lay down to sleep. She took the scraper, the one they use for cleaning skins, taking off the fleshy part, and went out. You know how they do it? They take a stick, a straight stick, lay the skins on a board and clean them.

The woman put on her hooded parka, did it up, and went out into the storm. The brothers lay there. "Look," said the youngest, "the storm has got quieter."

They listened carefully, and in fact it was quieter.

"I'm going out," said one of them.

"Stay where you are," said the oldest brother. The youngest said, "I'll just go out in the corridor."

"All right," said his elder brother, "but make sure you don't look anywhere."

That younger brother deceived his brothers. He looked around until he found a small hole in the yaranga cover and he looked out. He listened and heard "hrrrrr, hrrrrrr," like the sound of scraping skins. There he saw that woman sitting up in the sky cleaning it. In fact only a little bit of bad weather was left. The rest was all clear and light. The moon was shining and the weather was lovely.

The moment he saw her, she fell over!

He rushed away.

"What happened?" called the others. He ran and hid in a hole. In a moment—wham, she fell.

"Ohhh," groaned the woman. "You didn't obey me! I wanted to help you. I was trying to clear the weather for you. But I didn't have time to finish.

"If I had finished clearing the clouds, in the future you would always have had good weather. But as it is, you sometimes will have bad weather. Get home now while the weather is good. Even if it is the middle of the night."

The older brother scolded the younger, disobedient one.

"Get dressed, go," said the woman. They got ready fast. They went out and there was just a little cloud left in the sky. As they went along their way, everything melted. Then the wind started to blow. When they got close to their home, again such a storm came up!

Vaaii! The end.

Nakazik's voice is warm and rich, his turn of phrase in Russian humorous. He has a way of drawing you into his tale so that you can actually see the people and places. His style is in marked contrast to Lyuba's, though both are expert storytellers. Her telling has a hypnotic quality that delivers most of its message on an unconscious level, while to listen to Nakazik one must be very much awake, watching all the details.

He gave me the sense that he and I were the intelligent ones who understood how things work and were not fooled by anything. Then just as I was basking in this lovely feeling of being included, he would play a trick on me, forcing me to look at what was going on behind my back. It happened with the seal bones in the following story. I had to laugh at myself, enjoying his skill at making me see what he wanted me to see.

Two Brothers

This was long ago, as it always is in a story. In one yaranga there lived two families. On one side the younger brother lived with his family, and on the other side the elder brother, also with his family.

They were very successful hunters, and once in summer they went out hunting on a big baidara. I think it must have been August, because the evenings were getting dark and there might be rain. In the daytime it was sunny and warm.

They took off their parkas and rowed without them. They went a long distance. People used to be able to go hunting for two or three days at a time while the weather was good.

They came up to an island, and there on the island was a small hill. The younger brother jumped out and ran around the shore gathering driftwood to cook meat. He got everything ready and then looked around at his brother. The brother was sitting in the boat eating something.

"Come here and eat," called the younger brother. "I'm cooking fresh food."

"First I'll eat this dried meat and then I'll come to you."

"Why?"

He saw that his older brother was thinking, and then the older brother moved the boat farther from shore and left his younger brother there!

In the evening it began to rain, and it got cold. And he had no parka. Remember? He'd left it in the boat. He thinks, "What to do? There's nothing here on this island, nothing to eat. I may freeze and I may starve.

And even if I don't starve, the wild animals will kill me. I don't want to suffer," he decided. I must say here that hunter's knives were very long. He pulled out that big knife, waved it around, and got ready to kill himself.

Just as he was ready to plunge the knife in, he heard a voice saying, "Hey, what are you doing?"

"I must have imagined it," he thought. He raised the knife again.

Again came the voice, "Can a hunter really behave like that? A hunter never gives up. What kind of man are you?"

"I won't hurry to kill myself," he decided. He put the knife away, turned his back against the rain, and went to sleep, hungry but somewhat warmer.

He slept, and the sun started to shine brightly. And again he heard that voice. "Can a man really sleep that long?" it said. "You should get up and take a look on the shore."

So he went down, and there was a little seal warming itself in the sun. The man crept up, killed the seal, and ate his fill! He took the skin off, and in the course of the day it dried. Where the holes were for the paws, he was able to put his arms through. And when he had eaten, he didn't throw the bones away. He gathered all the bones together and laid them on the shore.

He stayed there and lived on the island.

From time to time that voice still scolded him—"You should be looking for tools," it said. As he walked around the edge of the island (after all, the island was small), he found a strong branch that he could use to make a bow. Then another time he found a pole and made a spear.

He went up the hill and found a hole. He made it deeper and then made a type of tent with some sticks. Then he started to shoot ducks—he didn't throw the skins away but kept them and dried them out. He laid them over the top of the tent and it became warm inside. He made some holes so he could look out and not scare the animals.

In the winter he looked out and saw that snow had fallen, and he saw a polar fox. He came out and shot the fox. And so he was able to make warmer clothes and to have a supply of food.

He spent the whole winter in this way. Then summer came again, the same time as before, exactly one year later. The man was getting ready to make a fire near his hut that day when he saw a point on the horizon.

He cut up some meat and looked again—it seemed to be closer. He looked again. "It must be a hunter," he thought.

He hid behind his hut and watched. Sure enough, it was a hunter coming closer—in fact it was his older brother! No parka—the weather was warm.

The older brother was thinking, "The winter was long and cold. He had no way to feed himself. He can't still be alive."

He came to the shore, got out of the boat, and then thought, "But what if he is alive? No! The winter was long, he had no clothes. Even if he didn't starve, the animals would have got him. Aha, there are his bones!"

Do you remember that seal? The bones had turned white. The older brother went up close and only then saw that they weren't human bones but seal. He turned around—and there sat his brother in the boat, eating!

"There you are!" says the older one. "I just couldn't live without my brother. I had to come back, at least to bury you. Come here, we'll eat together."

The younger answered the way his older brother had the year before. "First I'll eat a bit here, and then I'll come to you."

"Come here!" called the older brother again.

He had behaved so badly, leaving his younger brother to die!

The younger brother sailed away.

Evening came on the island, like the year before. Rain fell. The older brother was thinking, "How did he survive here? I can't do it."

And like his brother the year before, he took out his knife.

"Hey, what are you doing? Can a man really behave like that?" It was a good spirit talking. But no one appeared. Again the man picked up the knife, and again the voice came . . . but he went ahead and stabbed himself!

So we say, don't give in when bad things happen. All he would have had to do was to go up the hill. Everything was there! He could easily have lived.

The younger brother went home. People were happy to see him. He recognized his older brother's wife and saw that her children were clean.

Beside her was another woman. She was in terrible shape, thin, cut, and bruised. Her children were all ragged. This woman recognized her husband, the younger brother. She sat down and wept for joy.

This showed what a bad person that older brother was. He didn't help his brother's family and even cut her with a knife when preparing meat.

So in this story, evil was defeated! Fai! That's all.

The trick with the bones goes beyond just the fact that the older brother was fooled by them. Traditional wisdom says that if all of an animal's bones are left together in their correct order, the animal will gain new flesh and come back to life. But in this case it is the younger brother who has "come to life" by surviving when he might so easily have died. Nakazik makes a joke here by referring to a well-known belief, turning it to his own purpose. Like the man who wintered in the bear's den and the girl who wintered in the graveyard, this brother came back to his family against the odds.

On my return to Chaplino weeks later I found Nakazik at home with a handsome nephew. They were about to go out drinking, as they put it themselves. The occasion was honoring the passing of three years since the death of their uncle.

The nephew seemed to be in a hurry. But Nakazik agreed to tell just one more story. "He's a good storyteller!" said the nephew, and sat down to listen.

The magic of hair appears again in this story—the old woman awakens her power by combing her hair. There are some particularly dangerous evil spirits who attract people through sexuality. Here the young man survives by a kind of ruthlessness. The battle with the old woman is reminiscent of a shaman's competition and may indicate that he has supernatural aid as well as his own agility to thank for his survival.

The Evil Yaranga

There was a village, and right in the middle of it was a yaranga. Young men used to go in there and never be seen again. A girl lived there with her grandmother.

One day a young man went to their place. He went in and it was so light in the yaranga—two lamps burning in the sleeping room! It was warm and light. The grandmother was cutting up meat . . .

They ate, and when it was time to go to bed the grandmother lay down on one side of the sleeping room and these young people against the opposite wall.

He was beginning to fall asleep, but something began to bother him—something seemed suspicious. He opened his eyes part way. The old woman was sitting there—and looking right at him!

"All right," he thought, "I'll pretend to be asleep."

The old woman sat there—she sat there just looking at him. She went up to the one lamp that was burning. They had put one out for the night and made less fire in the other. She looked behind the lamp and took up her comb. They used to have little combs. She looked at the young man and combed her hair. As she combed one side, he pretended to be waking up. "Hmmm..."

The old woman threw herself onto her place and really went to sleep.

The young man said to his girl, "You know what, at home I'm used to sleeping beside the wall. I can't get to sleep like this." All right, so they traded places while the old woman was really sleeping.

"What are you doing? I'm going to marry this one," said the girl, scolding her mother when she thought he was asleep.

The man covered his head. After a while he lost his sleep. He looked through a crack between the wall and the skin he was sleeping under. He saw the old woman sit up, quickly go to the lamp, quickly comb her hair. Then she took her *olak,* a woman's knife kept in that place. She took up that knife threw it and cut off her daughter's head with the long braid— because they had traded places, you see.

"Ahh...because of you I have lost my daughter," she cried.

The fellow sat there—he had nothing to throw back at her. He returned the knife. The old woman said, "Because of you I lost my last daughter. You will not live."

She took the knife in her right hand and threw. He got out of the way and the knife went into the wood frame.

He took the knife in his right hand and threw it at her and cut off her right hand.

"All the same you will not live," she said.

She took the knife in her left hand, but he was agile and again he got out of the way.

"I'll show you how to throw," he said.

He took the knife in his left hand and threw it and cut off her left hand. Now she had no hands left.

"All the same you will not live," she said. She took the knife in her teeth, and how she threw it! The fellow just managed to get out of the way.

"I'll show you how to throw!"

Even though he had hands he took the knife in his teeth and threw it, cutting off the old woman's head! He began to get dressed. While all this had been going on, morning had come. It was getting light.

As he was getting dressed he saw that the yaranga with the room inside was getting lower and lower. He finished dressing and somehow just managed to get out before it sank completely away. He just managed to get his mitten through the door.

He looked back and the yaranga was gone.

He went home.

There used to be these holes in the skins of the sleeping room that you could look through. He looked in and saw his parents, sitting with their brows together, thinking, beginning to mourn, saying farewell to their son.

He coughed.

"That sounds like our son!"

"So it seems to me too!"

He coughed again.

"It's you!"

"It's me!"

They couldn't believe their luck.

"They let you go!"

And after that those evil spirits were no more.

That's all! Tfai![8]

By now Nakazik's nephew was willing to sit longer listening to stories. But Nakazik himself was ready to go. I said goodbye and went out and walked along the rocky shore, thoroughly chilled by the September wind, warmed by stories.

7 / Sireniki

Aglyu could tell without fail when it was worthwhile to go out hunting walrus. He refused to accompany the other hunters when he considered the conditions unfavorable—and he was always right! One time he arrived at Chaplino, twenty-five kilometers distant, in time to stand in the road and wave at the driver of a car that had left him standing at Providenia. No one knows how he was able to get there first!

—Alexandra Sokolovskaya

Days stretched long in Providenia with attempts to arrange transportation to the villages of Sireniki and Nunligran. It would have been ideal to go by boat, and it was possible that someone might come from Sireniki, three hours away by water, to get us. But the weather was chancy. There are many tragedies on the water every year, and no one wanted to risk the trip.

One day Svetlana and I walked to the tundra with Umryna, a local beadwork artist, to pick wild cranberries. Umryna took a small bucket and headed out along the only road from town—it leads around the bay to the airport, and a side road goes off to the left, over the hills to Chaplino. It took an hour to walk to this turn-off along the bumpy dirt road, frequently stepping aside to make room for passing trucks. We met a woman on the way who told us that just the week before she had met a white bear out there where we were going.

When we left the road to go into the tundra looking for berries, I couldn't believe this was the place Umryna had in mind. The ground was littered with junk: cans, bottles, rusting pieces of machinery, even an old shoe. Plant

Yupik beadwork artist Umryna picking berries outside Providenia.

life was tiny, hardly any richer than what I saw when I climbed in the rocks above the cemetery. But as we walked farther the debris thinned out, and Umryna started to find berries. You have to look carefully at first, but they are there.

Umryna got right to work and spent several hours bent over the ground, filling her small bucket. Svetlana and I had plastic bags, and we, too, worked industriously. As time passed I moved from frustration and disbelief at the difficulty of getting a winter's berries from such a sparse source to enjoyment in the hunt. I was delighted when I found a good stash, with big plump berries. Still, Svetlana and I wore out before Umryna, twenty years our senior.

She stopped with us for tea from the thermos and told us about her family. She was born in Kivak, a village that was liquidated in 1952. All the inhabitants were moved to the old village of Chaplino. Then a few years later they moved again—to New Chaplino. Two of her children were so unhappy in the new place that they ran away, back to Kivak. Four of Umryna's twelve children were buried in Kivak, but she remembers it as a good place to live. Everything was there, she says: good hunting, roots and berries easy to find. In Chaplino there was never enough to eat. After tea, Umryna went back to work as I admired the tundra flowers, some bright red spikes, others white balls of fluff.

Late in the day we walked back to town, buckets and bags full.

I checked books out of the library, and I walked the length of the town every day, from the cemetery at one end to the rows of tin garages at the other. I visited Chaplino again with Inuit young people from Canada, caught up on the Mexican soap operas that everyone watches on television, and transcribed all my tapes. I walked to the top of the hill behind the town and admired the magnificent scenery in the distance—fjords, mountains, tundra.

There are no movies or concerts in Providenia. Irina and Svetlana spent a lot of time looking out the windows, watching the ships come and go in the port. I was bored, compulsively worried about not getting enough done.

The most entertaining way of passing the time in Providenia was dropping in at the museum for tea, which could be had almost any time. Alexandra Sokolovskaya told fascinating tales of her forty years teaching and working in the area and of her difficulties in trying to move back to central Russia now that she was ready to retire. The administration had offered her an apartment in a city where she had never lived and knew no one. She was trying to negotiate a trade in order to live in the same city as her son.

Alla recalled stories that her mother, Ainana, told about shamans.

"She was young, and her brother got sick. They called in a Chukchi shaman. Inside a dark yaranga she was told to hold one side of a skin parka, and another girl the other. They were told not to investigate the proceedings. The shaman began to drum and sing, and the parka jumped around, dancing. Ainana looked up into the sleeve to see if he was cheating. It was empty. Then he stopped and said to take the girl [Ainana] away because she didn't believe. He knew."

And this about Aglyu, the husband of Kevutkak—one of the women with tattoos we had met in Chaplino. One time he was drunk, and the police locked him in a barn. Later he was seen walking around the village.

"One time my grandfather dropped his pipe in Imtuk Lake, near Sireniki," said Alla. "He was very fond of that pipe and sorry to lose it. Aglyu came to visit and sang with his drum in the darkened house. When they put the lights back on, there was the pipe under his chair!

"Another time a man had no bullets, and Aglyu made some appear. He said the mice helped.

"Yet another time Ainana was sitting in the yaranga sewing. Aglyu came in and told her to go look in the corridor at the walrus skull. (They never threw them away but kept them to help with future hunts. A skull kept in the corridor would attract the spirit of another walrus.) She looked at the skull and its mouth was snapping open and shut. Ainana had been sewing, cutting out slippers on a board. He made the board rise up into the air and fly around.

"He probably healed too, but in general they say that those who do very showy things can't heal. Skill was passed from father to son. And from mother to daughter.

"Early one morning two young men set off to go hunting. Shortly after they left, the shaman came by asking after one of them. But he had already gone. That day rocks fell from the cliff and both young men were wounded. One went for help. The one who waited froze to death. Later that shaman said that he had come by so early to warn them not to go."

The way women worked was more subtle. "When my sister Olya was sick in the hospital," said Alla, "a certain elderly woman taught my aunt a special charm to whisper in her ear. My aunt came and whispered in Olya's ear and she got better. But after that my aunt could never remember the words again. We think the old woman made it that way on purpose, so that it would work only one time."

Alexandra Sokolovskaya said, "Shamans are called in to find out the proper name for a child, which means they must find out who has returned in the form of this child. Thus it can happen that a boy gets a girl's name or vice versa. Sometimes people change their names after an illness. This still happens today. There are people who can be called in to find out the name; it's not a big *kamlanie* [ceremony]. Even young people today may be doing it."

Eventually Alla and Alexandra had to get back to work, and I would go for another walk, read another book.

But this particular morning I walked into the museum and Alla said, "There you are. You can have a ride to Sireniki if you are ready to go in half an hour." A military truck was taking provisions (which didn't take up much room) and a group of Yupik missionaries from St. Lawrence Island. Alla would call ahead and arrange a place for me to stay when I got there.

I rushed home, threw a toothbrush into my camera bag, and donned my long underwear. It would take about five hours, Alla said, in the open back of the truck. Svetlana decided to come too, in spite of the danger to her eyes in riding over the bumpy road.

We piled into the truck with the people from the American side, who provided a striking contrast to their Asian relatives in their relative prosperity. They were dressed in bright jackets and baseball caps.

We left the town in a convoy of two—one truck never makes the trip alone. The danger in case of a breakdown is too great: no radios or cellular phones. We turned off the road to Chaplino near the berry-picking place and crossed a range of hills to a small ferry that crossed the other arm of the bay on which Providenia is located.

From the other side we went up into the tundra, along what was no longer a road but a creek bed. I was frequently glad that we were in the back, with a view of where we had been rather than of what was ahead. There were sheer drop-offs and huge rocks; we forded small rivers and slogged through mud. I soon got bruised from bouncing on the wooden bench. Luckily Svetlana's eyes survived undamaged.

The scenery was magnificent, and I wish we had stopped bumping long enough to look at it. The hills alternated red, green, white, and gold. Lovely marsh grasses swayed in the wind, topped with white feathers.

But the trip was long. In fact it took more than seven hours to reach Sireniki, and we arrived after dark, exhausted. Nina Notai, who runs the local House of Culture, met us and took us home to dinner and bed.

The next day we looked at the village. Its setting is spectacular—the beach is framed on both ends with dramatic rock cliffs, a river rushes into the sea, and the tundra stretches yellow into the distance, dotted with white bones. A new walrus-skin boat was being built on the shore. Men sat on the cliff with binoculars early in the morning, watching the sea for whales or walrus. But they saw few, and people in the village were very poor. There was practically nothing to eat. Nina has some relatives in the tundra, so she had a little reindeer meat, but supplies in the village were almost nonexistent. In the store there were two very expensive bananas and literally nothing else. There was a lot of tuberculosis in Sireniki; resistance to disease was low. Not long ago, I heard, someone got a sack of buckwheat that had been treated with poison to kill rats. The dealer sold the buckwheat in Sireniki, and many people became severely ill—someone may even have died of it.

Over tea, Nina told me about her grandfather, who was a shaman. "He died in 1973," she said, "and now there are no shamans in Sireniki. He should have passed the gift to a relative, but he didn't. He made drums and *pelikens*

The beach and rock cliffs at Sireniki. There is a similar cliff at the other end of the beach, recalling the image of the clashing rocks in Nununa's tale of the woman who married a whale.

[ivory amulets], and people consulted him about hunting. He had four amulets—one from the first fox he killed, a white bear claw, a walrus tusk, and something from a wolf—I forget what part. Grandfather would go down the river alone with the person who was sick—and next day the person would get better. When I was eight years old he healed me. I was often sick as a child, but this time they thought I had died. He brought me back from the other world. It took several days. What I remember is that it felt as if he were shaking me. Then I got better."

Nina's mother, Sivugun, showed us her tattoos. Yupik designs are more intricate than those of the Chukchi. Sivugun said that her tattoos were done in 1925, when she was about ten years old, by her girlfriend Kaksyaka, who was three years older. They did it as a lark, and her parents were angry when they saw them.

One of Sivugun's neighbors told about how she learned to hunt. Panana

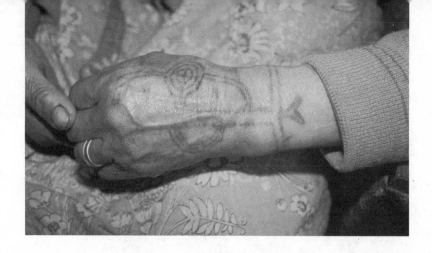

Sivugun's hand tattoos, done when she was a young girl. The deisgns are very similar to those recorded by Bogoras a century before.

remembered that she was not allowed to go hunting until she had her tattoos. She grew up with no brothers, and so she should have been allowed to hunt with her father. But even when her face was done, the men did not want her to go hunting, and so she went in secret. She developed a reputation for her strength and bravery. Her family kept the store in Sireniki, and she was the one who regularly rowed a walrus-skin *baidara* the three hours to Providenia in all kinds of weather for supplies.

Another of Sireniki's most respected elders was Nununa, and we visited her next.

She was born in 1907 in the nearby village of Imtuk, she said, in a *yaranga*. They used to gather grass and cover the house with mud. Oil lamps were small but cooked everything. It got hot indoors from the lamp. They made the lamp base of clay. At Imtuk they had birds and fish, but no freshwater. So they had to move to Sireniki. There was a spit, with a lake beyond it. When the seawater washed over the spit, the fish came in on the big waves, as if the lake were opening and closing.

In 1994 Nununa was one of only two people who remembered any of the old Sireniki dialect. Nowadays people in Sireniki speak the Chaplino dialect. This is interesting because Sireniki is one of the few villages that have not changed location; it has existed for hundreds of years or more on this rocky shore. On the other hand, the people of Naukan have retained their dialect but lost their village. The change came about as people from

For the Yupik woman Panana, receiving her facial tattoos represented a coming of age.

Chaplino moved into Sireniki, leading to the disintegration of the Sireniki tribe. Government policies of printing the Yupik language as spoken in Chaplino further weakened the Sireniki dialect.[1]

Nununa sang several songs in the Sireniki dialect, and I was surprised to learn that one of them was not a very old song—indeed, it was about the Soviet astronaut Yuri Gagarin, who in April 1961 became the first man to orbit the earth. In light of stories about flying shamans, I began to see the astronaut's accomplishments differently!

Nununa explained how her facial tattoos were done. All the girls tattooed each other as they approached puberty. Nununa said that the designs on her right hand were done by her older sister, and those on the left hand by someone else.

They used black soot from a cooking pot mixed with seal fat and applied it using a needle and thread. Although it was very painful, they claim it was

Nununa, one of the last two speakers of the Sireniki dialect of the Yupik language.

done simply "for beauty." I looked at sketches made a hundred years earlier by Waldemar Bogoras and saw exactly the same intricate designs.[2] Alla Panaug'ye says that in earlier times the tattoos were believed to give protection from evil spirits and to ensure fertility, but nobody thinks of them in that way any more. In the past, some men had tattoos as well, although they were never as elaborate as those of the women.[3]

I asked Nununa for a story, and following is the tale she told. Even her niece, Nina Notai, said she had never heard Nununa tell it before. Nina translated it from Yupik into Russian.

The Girl Who Married a Whale

It was long ago, when we were not here yet—when everything was not yet developed, the land had just started to breathe.

Some girls went down on the shore with the young men and there they all married. But the numbers were uneven and one girl didn't get a husband. There was a whale bone on the beach with a hole in it, and the girl's foot got caught there. The others pulled and pulled but they couldn't pull her out. They went away to call for help. The bone started moving toward the sea and took the girl with it. Her mother and father came to try to save her. Her brothers came, too, but they saw that she was far away out at sea.

The brothers went to look for her. And when they were getting ready to get in their boat, there were some birds. I don't know what they're called—they fly very fast. The parents said, "If you see those birds going somewhere, then you go there too."

Then the birds flew by—they are small, with sharp wings. Quickly the young men got the boat ready and set off after the birds. Along the way there were two moving rock cliffs. They open apart and crash closed. The brothers succeeded in getting through, following the birds, and then the rocks clapped shut.

They went along, following the shoreline. After a while the oldest brother looked up and said, "It looks as if there is something alive up there. Let's go look."

They went up and there was their sister, already pregnant.

"Come home with us," they said.

"No, I won't go with you," she replied, "I have a husband now, the whale."

All the same, they took her.

She wept.

Again they just managed to get past those moving rocks. They looked back and saw a big whale swimming after them. They got ready and watched the flock of birds. They didn't fly but sailed quickly through.

They got back to their own shore, and there the girl gave birth to a baby whale.

At first she kept him in a big bathing tub. She fed him when he called her. But he didn't turn into a human. When he started to grow they kept him in a lagoon that they dug, and there he swam.

Then he got to be a year old. They let him go into the sea. His father swam up often to look at him.

Whale bones on the shore outside Providenia.

This son had a sort of talisman attached near his eye. And when they went hunting, the people didn't touch those whales, neither the son nor the father.

But then some people came from another settlement and killed the baby whale. The mother worried, she saw it happening. These people came and began cutting up the whale on the beach. The mother came up and saw the talisman. When nothing was left but bones, she gathered them and pressed them together and slept with them.

That father whale overturned the boat of those hunters as they were leaving. All of them died who had killed that boy-whale.

That's all. You see what cruelty there was.

Tauwa.

There are many stories along the shore of people who marry sea mammals, and the story of the woman and the whale is one of the most frequently heard. It also appears in Menovshchikov's Eskimo collection, with several differences. In that version it is the whale's skull that carries the girl away, and the clashing rocks are located near the whale's home. When the brothers arrive, the whale enters into a shamanic competition with them. The sister helps her brothers, and they make their escape. On the way back she removes her articles of clothing one by one and throws them back to the whale, which slows him down long enough for her and her brothers to get home. This version says that the baby whale brought other whales to shore who volunteered their bodies to the hunters. After the baby was killed, the mother's tears cleaned his bones.[4]

As a story is retold in new geographic locations, tellers add and subtract details. The unique feature of Nununa's version is the crashing rocks, which bring to mind the rocks on the beach at Sireniki or the lake at Imtuk, which seemed to open and close as water rushed over the spit. On Sireniki beach, the big cliffs that rise majestically on either end look as if they could crash together, and if they did, they would fit together perfectly. On the beach at Sireniki those little birds can be seen darting quickly this way and that. A person who can read their movements will know exactly when to take the boat out, perhaps avoiding other rocks in the bay. The image of clashing rocks is familiar in stories of a quest, as in Homer's *Odyssey*. I have also heard it told as part of a shaman's journey among the Khakass of south-central Siberia.

The image of marriage with an animal is basic to understanding the place of humanity in nature. It acknowledges the intimate connection between people and the animals they depend on. The results of the marriage are frequently tragic, especially for the animal.

When human women marry land animals, such as bears and tigers in the Amur region, they give birth to both animal and human children who often survive to found new clans. We might expect that to happen here, and Nununa acknowledges the possibility by saying, "He did not turn into a human." But those who marry whales give birth only to whales, and the babies die. Whereas stories about land animals tell of people's origins, tales of sea mammals tell of hunting taboos.[5]

141

A much-quoted Iglulik Eskimo shaman said to the explorer Knud Rasmussen in the 1920s, "The greatest peril of life lies in the fact that human food consists entirely of souls. All the creatures that we have to kill and eat, all those that we have to strike down and destroy to make clothes for ourselves, have souls that do not perish with the body and which must therefore be (pacified) lest they should revenge themselves on us for taking away their bodies."[6] A good part of human activity had to do with gaining an element of control in this relationship with nature, but it was control through understanding and balance rather than control through destruction.

The story of the woman and the whale expresses the tragedy involved in this dilemma, and the solution. People must kill to live, but by obeying the laws of nature they ensure that their killing is not permanent and that the animals return and stay in balance. This is expressed in the story by the fact that the woman sleeps with the bones, an image that appears as the jumping-off point in other stories of resurrection. Bones are connected with shamanic death and rebirth, as is the possibility that the boys might have flown when returning with their sister. They didn't turn into birds, as a shaman might have done, but followed the birds.

In order to stay in balance, certain animals must not be killed at all—in this case the whale marked with the talisman given to it by the woman who was its mother. The foreigners who disobeyed this taboo, even through ignorance, were severely punished for it. Life in the Arctic is a precarious balance indeed.

There is a frustrating sense of dead-end in this story, as there is in the legend about the girl who wintered in the graveyard. Chukchi and Yupik beliefs are full of cycles of death and rebirth, but these stories end with death and only hint at rebirth. The cycle has been interrupted. The moral about hunting taboos may have been added onto the earlier story of female creative power that is brought to a halt with the death of the baby whale.

After hearing Nununa's story, we made plans for the next day—to visit another grandmother who had not been feeling well, and to hear more about how walrus-skin boats were made. In the evening a young Russian man came by who wanted to sell baleen and illegally acquired archaeological objects.[7] I was outraged. Such things belong in place, I said; many of those sites are sacred. At least the things belong in a museum and not on the black market. Svetlana was uncomfortable with my talking like that.

Economic desperation leaves no room for this kind of moralizing. She turned to eliciting the young man's story.

She heard about his Yupik wife, who was depressed and drinking heavily, and his concerns for his two daughters. Svetlana promised to send the girls a watermelon from Providenia, where such exotic things could be had.

Our plans for the next day did not come to be. During the night a man died—not an old man, not a fighter or a drinker, but a good working man in his early forties. He died of an unexpected heart attack. The entire village was going into mourning, and we suddenly felt we were in the way. When we learned that the trucks were going back, we went.

Unfortunately, this was not the last death. During my last ten days in Providenia a man was murdered up on the hill after a drunken argument, two boys died in a car crash, and the wife of the young Russian we had met in Sireniki committed suicide by disembowelling herself. One of the bay ferries overturned because a piece of heavy equipment was loaded improperly, likely by drunken ferry workers. Nine people on board died in the icy water, while one was rescued by his dog. Each day we came to dread what horrifying thing might happen next. I was ready to go home.

Luckily, these last few days were enriched by my quick visit to Nunligran and my meetings with Galina Tagrina.

8 / Nunligran

My name means "The one who will carry on the songs."
—Galina Tagrina

I had heard glowing reports of the village of Nunligran from Svetlana Chuklinova on my first day in Providenia. Svetlana said that when I got to Nunligran, which she had no doubt I would do, I must be sure to meet Galina Nikolaevna Tagrina, composer, poet, singer, dancer, and master of the art of embroidering with the chin hairs of a reindeer. Tagrina has long been the leader of Nunligran's performing ensemble, and she was Svetlana's own mentor.

Weeks later I had almost given up on Nunligran because of transportation difficulties. Then, on the very evening we got back from Sireniki, Irina's husband came home from his work on the ships saying I could go to Nunligran that night aboard the ship that delivered diesel fuel to run the electric station. It normally didn't take passengers, but he would take me aboard.

The trip out took nine hours, and I slept most of the time in the captain's comfortable upper berth while he was on duty. I got up in time to watch the rocky coastline as we approached Nunligran.

These are the kinds of rocks that inspire storytellers, I thought. They are dramatic—sharp and jutting, in colors ranging from cold Arctic grays to red, green, and gold. One looked to me like a woman huddled in the water holding a baby, and others seemed to have been thrown there in a big hurry by a passing giant.

As we approached Nunligran I was struck by the litter of rusting forty-five-gallon drums on the shore. Left behind from an earlier system of diesel

Chukchi artist Ivan Nagalyuk with his three granddaughters and the
author (on right).

delivery, they are a common sight in the tundra as well. Next to them stand
the gigantic bones of whales that have been brought up on this shore over
the years—their vertebrae, long skulls, and wide shoulder blades look pre-
historic in contrast with the rusty metal.

The boat was pulled up onto the beach by tractors, and I got off riding
piggy-back on the shoulders of a man who sloshed through thigh-deep
water in big rubber boots.

The village—mostly old wooden houses—was set back from the pebble
beach, where a ferocious wind was blowing. I had only a few hours in Nunligran—enough to visit Chukchi artist Ivan Nagalyuk, who came out to meet
the boat with his two granddaughters, and to find out that Galina Tagrina
was away on vacation.

Ivan Nagalyuk was born in the area of Lake Avan, between Sireniki and
Nunligran. He learned the arts of carving, engraving, and making minia-
tures from his father and uncles. He made miniature versions of all the

Iulia Nagalyuk and a doll she made with the help of her grandfather.

traditional goods of the Chukchi—sleighs, walrus-skin boats, bone carvings, dolls in reindeer-skin clothing. He was teaching these arts to his grand-daughters, who already made excellent dolls. He described the place of art-work in their economic life.

"On hunting and fishing trips there was always a lot of time spent wait-ing, for the weather or the animals. During that time we made things. Before the Soviet times, American, French, Norwegian, English, Japanese, and even Canadian ships used to come around here. We traded gifts and souvenirs with them, and lived from that trade.

"Ships used to come and get freshwater from a stream that flows into Vsadnik Bay. Yupik people came down to meet the ships at Chaplino and Kivak, Sireniki, and other places. They made sealskin bags and other things. In trade they received tobacco, sugar, flour, fabric, and tea. My grandfather taught me to make the little baidaras. That and the sleighs are the most complex to make. The rest is easy. The dolls were my own idea—carving the

Precisely detailed model of a *baidara* and rower by Ivan Nagalyuk.

face is the most complicated part." Nagalyuk lived in Nunligran until his death in 1995.

I arrived back in town another nine hours later and slightly the worse for wear from the rolling of the boat. The trip had been worthwhile for the scenery and for seeing Nagalyuk's work. But there had been no stories other than the ones I made up myself.

Next morning I went to visit my friend Alla at the museum. "There you are," she said. "Tagrina is in town at her daughter's. I'll take you over there."

And so we went. On the way, Alla explained that Galina Nikolaevna had been away in Irkutsk—on a vacation that must have felt tropical to a person from Chukotka. Now she was at her daughter's apartment, waiting for a helicopter to Nunligran. At last the difficulties of Russian transport were playing into my hands. The woman was stranded here!

Alla introduced me briefly—"This is Kira from Canada. She's interested in stories and music."

And then she was gone. But by now I was used to Alla.

Tagrina walked slowly, owing to a severe case of arthritis in her feet. We went down the corridor and out into the living room, which was chaotic with boxes and cleaning—the apartment had been rented out in their absence.

"I suppose we should have tea," she said, and called her grandson to make it. We squeezed into the kitchen.

She asked me questions about myself, which, in my work, surprisingly few people do. She learned that I had gone into folklore collecting after

Chuckchi musician, composer, and artist Galina Tagrina. Providenia.

twenty years as a professional cellist. Also that I had been in Anadyr the previous year and had made friends with some of her relatives there, Lena Naukeke and Viktor Tymnev'ye.

I learned that she had been married to a Ukrainian and that the marriage had failed over her inability to adjust when he wanted to go back to Ukraine to live. She just had not been able to get used to the food—she kept on longing for fresh walrus meat. With a twinkle in her eye she said, "You probably wouldn't like it." She parted company with her husband after several journeys back and forth between Ukraine and Chukotka. Because I suspected that my own marriage was rapidly heading in the same direction, we had already found two points in common—music and divorce.

The whole sense of these few moments was that we were both aware of the beginning of a potentially interesting relationship and were feeling out where to start. We were both stuck in Providenia with little to do, and there was plenty of time. In a situation like this a new friendship can be the best way to fill it. I thought of what a rarity that would be in the society I live in, where there is always some form of entertainment. In Providenia there is nothing but friends. Tagrina knows a lot more about this than I do, I thought. I also had a sense of having passed a test, mainly because of my cello. She, too, had devoted most of her life to music.

"Well, you probably think I'm terribly rude for asking you these questions," she said, turning to check my face to see whether or not this was so.

"Not at all," I answered, "I'm glad you are interested."

"Anyhow, we will get to know each other. I will tell you about myself first." We went back to the living room and made ourselves comfortable.

"I am not a storyteller. I am a musician. I will sing you some songs, but not today. Now I could tell you about my family name. Are you interested?"

"Yes, please."

"My father was from Enmelen. There people pronounce 'ah'; in Nunligran, 'eh.'"

It took me a while to realize that the whole story that follows would explain why people in the two villages pronounced this sound differently.

"My mother was from Uel'kal, from the tundra. I learned sewing from my mother and songs from my father. My personal song, given to me by my father, means 'One who carries on the songs.' My father's clan was called Tuptek. He used to gather singers from all over for holidays. It wasn't like now, part of some cultural program. That was just what he did. People used to pass by on boats or on dogsleds and they all stopped at our place and sang. My mother spent a lot of her time making the things that were given out as prizes—clothing, boots, things like that.

"There's a family legend about the man called Tuptek. He was our ancestor, so long ago that nobody knows for sure how long. Do you know what Tuptek means? I'll draw a picture. This is a sealskin. You know, they use them for floats in the water. Then around where the neck of the seal was, they tie a cord and there's a little stick on the end of the cord and that stick is called *tuptek*. I don't know why that was the man's name.

"Tuptek's people were poor. And so he traveled to Uel'kal to find a wife among the Yupik people, because he was too poor to find a wife among the rich people where he lived. There at Uel'kal he found a girl to marry. She was her father's only daughter. She had been married several times but each time the man sent her back because she didn't give birth to any children. Tuptek said he would marry her anyway. The father was delighted that his childless daughter would have a husband. And the father asked the young man, 'Do you have something you believe in? What are your beliefs?' And the young man said, 'No, I have none.'"

Here the story stopped. It was clear that this tale was not thought out for the telling. She had to decide how to go on. She explained that we weren't talking about anything like Christian beliefs. I realized that. But still, where to pick up the thread? "It's a long story," she said. "I'd better go back."

I waited.

"You see, as a child he had been the only survivor when everyone else around him starved. In those days there were no boundaries for pasturing reindeer. People moved around. One group went deep into the Anadyr region to a forested tundra area for a period of three or four years. They needed to leave the land around Enmelen to heal itself because there was nothing left for the reindeer to eat. They moved in a big caravan, taking everything with them, reindeer, yarangas—everything. When they came back they would bring poles for yarangas, wood for sleighs. They traded for these things using seal oil, straps made of sea lion skin, boot soles of walrus and sea lion.

"Meanwhile, there was a very bad winter while they were gone. The strongest people had been left behind in Enmelen. They were the richest, too. The poorer people, who had gone away to the forest tundra, came back three years later. They found that all the people who had stayed behind had died. People were still lying there in the yarangas along the shore as if they were sleeping—no one had even buried them.

"The returning nomads came to the last yaranga. There, too, the people were all dead except for this one little boy. He was barely alive and had only two or three teeth. He had fed himself from his dead mother's breast. That was the boy Tuptek.

"And so those people from the tundra took him along and brought him up. But they always told him, 'You are not one of us. Go back to Enmelen and live there.' And so when he grew up he went there and set himself up, but he had no one to learn beliefs and traditions from.

"When he went to Uel'kal looking for a wife, the girl's father said, 'Since you are taking my daughter, I will teach you knowledge of our beliefs and holidays.' And so the old man taught the young one. And the young man took the girl home, and later that childless woman gave birth to four children! That was long ago—so long that it's almost become a legend.

"When Yupik people speak Chukchi they say 'ah' instead of 'eh.' At first people at Enmelen teased that Yupik woman about her pronunciation, but later they picked it up. This is why people in Enmelen speak the way they do. My name Tagrina would be Tegrine in 'correct' Chukchi. My father's name was Ritagrau, which means something like 'Coming down from the sky.' Tegrinteu is the same. That's because that Yupik woman's family prayed to Mars and brought gifts to that planet."

Quite a saga from a person who is not a storyteller! We returned to the room from this journey through the Chukotka of the past. I had actually been seeing the reindeer caravan, the boy starving among his dead relatives, the young woman being teased for her speech. Now the conversation wound down.

I asked Tagrina about her Russian name. Chukchi people used to have only one name, but with the coming of Soviet power most had taken on Russian first names and patronymics and kept their Chukchi names as family names. But nobody had ever told me how the Russian names were selected.

At the time Galina Nikolaevna was born, in November 1936, Russian traders came to the village saying that shamanism must be wiped out. Her father was accused of being a shaman because of all his singing and the holidays he put on. These traders warned him. They told him to leave, so he took the family and moved farther away from the village, about twelve kilometers down the coast. They lived there for a number of years.

Before they left, one trader looked at the newborn girl. He said, "When she gets to be seven years old, I will take her." The father didn't want to give his daughter up, but he agreed. After all, seven years is a long time. And of course he never did give her up. The trader gave the girl her name and patronymic. Galina was the name of his wife, and Nikolai was his own name.

Her father took the trader's name, Nikolai Petrovich. And then they moved away. Friends and relatives helped them and visited during their years of exile from Enmelen. His whole family was physically very strong; people sent their sons to him for training in sports, weight lifting, races, and jumping. There wasn't so much alcohol then. When they were invited to Naukan for competitions, far away in the tundra, they ran there. At these holidays the shore people and the tundra people traded by means of an exchange of gifts.

I wasn't sure whether I should ask the next question. People in Chukotka don't talk much about shamans—not only because of the repressions of the Stalinist years, I believe, but because they never did talk much about them. Some things are better not talked about. The talk dilutes the power. The same is true of dreams. Most of the stories that I do hear about shamans are about the very showy things some of them used to do, not the private world of spirituality.

I took a deep breath. "Was he actually a shaman, your father?"

"He sang. I remember his telling me, there are bad shamans who can cast spells and kill people, and good shamans who can heal people. I saw that he healed people."

This was the way she continued to talk about her father. Other people also talked about shamans (if that's what they were) in this way. There were just some people who could heal, and others who could tell what the weather and the hunting would be like, and people called them when they needed them.

It was getting late. We agreed that I would come back the next day and record some songs.

But the next day Galina Nikolaevna had a headache, and her daughters had turned the apartment upside down to get rid of cockroaches and put things in order. Could we record the next day, and try to find a place that would be quieter, with fewer children indoors and passing trucks outdoors? I'd try, I said.

That afternoon I chatted with Alexandra Sokolovskaya at the museum, who also wanted to record the songs. Her apartment faced away from the street and had no children on a regular basis. We made plans.

That night I started to imagine what this meeting would be like. These two women, now in their late fifties, had probably known each other for many years. Both were active in Chukotka's cultural scene. Sokolovskaya had come from central Russia as a young woman and spent forty-three years working in the Providenia region, teaching several generations of schoolchildren in a series of village schools. For the last ten years she had been the force behind the creation and growth of the Providenia museum. Now on the verge of retirement to a government apartment in a city in Russia where she knew nobody, she was looking back over her memories. She is a woman with a profound respect for the traditional culture of the Chukchi and Yupik peoples. It was she who had walked me through the museum exhibits, filling in interesting anecdotes about most of them. She also has firmly held opinions and a loud voice.

Alexandra Sokolovskaya warned that Galina Nikolaevna was a fascinating woman, but with the temperament of an artiste, a word she filled with disdain. I looked forward to the meeting with the two of them because of their long years of contact and also because, at the age of forty-eight, I found myself increasingly enjoying the company of women older than myself. The dynamic seemed to be that I was still young enough for them to want to fill me in on things, yet old enough that they did not watch their language or hold their tongues on subjects such as teenagers or men.

So I went over to collect Tagrina at the appointed time, after lunch. She and her two daughters and three grandchildren were all squeezed into the kitchen eating walrus meat, which had somehow been found in Providenia. Tagrina was noticeably less homesick for Nunligran than the day before.

"You wouldn't want any," she said breezily, "but you can have tea." Immediately the two daughters picked up the table and carried it into the living room, and we all had tea. It turned out that there was an increasing possibility (or danger, from my point of view) of a helicopter in two more days. This was really good news for her, because sometimes you can wait a month for a ride.

Tagrina got into her heavy support boots and took her cane in hand, and we started off. It took quite a while to get to Sokolovskaya's, up the hill and then up to the fourth floor. Once there, we soon got our little recording studio set up in yet another small kitchen. I was right about the interplay between the two women—Tagrina critiqued Sokolovskaya constantly on her smoking and her seeming inability to keep quiet while the tape recorder was on. Sokolovskaya gave back as good as she got, commenting on the fussiness of the artiste. There were sudden stops in the recording owing to some slight or insult that I had not perceived.

And just when everything got quiet, the refrigerator kicked in. If we opened the window to get rid of the cigarette smoke, we heard trucks from the street. There were a few digs from the artiste—saying pointedly to me, "You know, I told you about that already," letting it be known that I had inside information. Although most of this was probably friendly sparring, there was an undercurrent if not of animosity then of resentment over the relations between the peoples. On the one hand, there was the resentment of the native person whose culture has been devastated by contact with Russian power and whose personal life is fraught with the problems of mixed marriage and childrearing. On the other hand, Sokolovskaya had devoted her whole working life to education in native communities, helping many young people on to higher education. And now here was the artiste sharing information with some upstart from Canada who had just arrived. It was not easy to be neutral in this situation.

Tagrina sang twelve songs that afternoon. She began with a whole series of personal songs, first her father's in two versions. One she remembered from childhood, and the other was as he corrected her later in life. Then we heard the personal songs of Tagrina and each of her three siblings. The oldest sister had a song called "Little Sun," because as the first child she brought sunlight to the lives of her parents. The second child was a son, and his song says that he will be strong and independent. Tagrina herself was third, with a song for the one who will carry on the songs. The fourth child, also a girl, lived only a few months; her song called her little mosquito—I don't know why.

Tagrina's personal songs reminded me of the childhood names and songs other Chukchi friends had told me about. Every Chukchi child used to receive a special name in childhood that referred either to a characteristic of the child or to something that happened at the time of birth. I had met "Woman who goes straight forward"—Valentina Itevtegina, "Woman who goes around things"—Katia Reultineut, and "The dog came back"—Svetlana Chuklinova. Part of the reason for these names is the habit of *not* calling the child by her real name until she is old enough to resist the evil spirits that will be attracted to its sound. People talked of calling a shaman or an older relative to discover which deceased ancestor had come back in the form of the newborn child, so that the appropriate name could be given. This was still being done—Lena Naukeke in Tavaivaam was one person who could do it.

Most of my earlier Chukchi acquaintances composed their own personal songs later in life. But in the case of Tagrina's family, the songs seem to have been given by their father at birth, complete with melody and lyrics. This is one of those things I wish I had asked about—why this difference? But I didn't put it all together until afterward—the interplay between the songs and the names, personal characteristics, weather conditions at the time of birth, and the transmigration of souls. I remember Katia Reultineut in Anadyr saying that where she was from, people didn't ask, "Who are you?" but instead, "Whose are you?" The names give that picture.

All the "real" names within Tagrina's family are related but not the same: father Ritagrau, first daughter Tagrinaut, son Tigrinkeo, daughter Tagrina, and youngest child Tagrit. These are all variations on "Coming down from the sky," referring back to that Yupik woman, the wife of Tuptek.

Tagrina reflected on the songs given at birth and how life had worked out for those people. Her brother, who was to be strong and independent, did in fact turn out that way—at least until things went wrong for him later. As for herself—"The songs are left with her"—her whole life until recently had been devoted to music. How did her father know that? she wondered. "But they say he was a shaman—that means he knows where it came from!" Now she is laughing about her father's being a shaman. It's a serious business, yet a lot of funny situations arose from it too. I also took this to mean that I was trusted a degree further than the day before.

An amazing connection happened at this point. For some reason I told her then about the fact that after twenty years of professional music—a passion I had expected to last my whole life—a few years ago the interest had started to wane. Now I played hardly at all and a new passion had taken its place. Her jaw dropped nearly to her chest. "It's the same for me," she said. "Years and years it was all music—I thought it would be forever. And now I hardly sing, and spend most of my time sewing and embroidering." This is a thing few people truly understand, even my closest friends at home. Those who don't play themselves, or do something they relate to the same way, can't see how what I do with music now is different from what I did before. Those are the ones who don't know the pain that accompanies the pleasure and sometimes eclipses it. Nor do they know the totality of the involvement. Musicians, on the other hand, don't see how that relationship could stop, thinking this is just a phase I'm going through. With Tagrina I suddenly felt totally at home about this, crossing the distance from my own world to this one so far away.

From this point on the nature of our contact became more intimate, and Tagrina's competitive digs at Sokolovskaya got sharper. "Move back, Alexandra Grigorievna, you are making a narrow path for the songs!" she said, implying that the other woman, in her boldly striped sweater, was taking up too much space in a small room. "Why do you smoke so much? We are not fish, to be preserved in smoke!"

Tagrina's voice is powerful and rich. The afternoon wore on and it started to get dark. A grandson stopped by for a key. We heard songs from Tagrina's grandfather Aipentenmau, who also sang a lot. There were songs that many men sang together. There was a song for the girls of that place where Tuptek's clan lived, called Silalren. And a special song for a place out on the spit where the holidays were held.

Tagrina's grandfather had a brother who also used to put on big holidays and sang a lot. But when Tagrina's father, Ritagrau, got stronger in singing, his uncle stopped. Whether or not these men were shamans in the sense used by anthropologists, they had the power of song. I recalled the story of Tsaimygyryn, whose power increased as he sang. This power is recognized by Tagrina in the idea of not making a narrow path for the song. At the end of the afternoon she looked me in the eye (I was sitting directly opposite her across a small table) and said, "You must be tired from sitting there receiving all those songs." I was!

She mentioned another uncle who was accused of being a shaman. "But I saw him alive. Arkam didn't shamanize, didn't heal anyone, didn't kill anyone, he just sang very much! The thing I like about his song is that there is something Yupik in it and something Chukchi."

The words and melodies of personal songs may change over the course of a person's life. They are still the same songs, but different—in her father's case, simpler. Tagrina is interested in what kinds of changes there are and how they come about. She emphasizes that she doesn't sing all the songs she knows in a systematic way but works into her repertoire the ones she likes best. This is almost an apology, but also just normal behavior on the part of a performing artist.

At last Tagrina explained how she began to write her own songs. "The interest began late. I sang that song with my father in childhood, but as far as making anything up—that came later. I worked and traveled when I was taken away from my studies. They said my veins were going bad all over my body. I was in boarding school in Providenia. [This is where she complained that the food was so bad.] A doctor came from Anadyr and told my father that if he wanted me to live he must take me away from the school to a place where it would be quiet. 'She must not look at books for three years,' he said.

And so my father took me to the tundra and I worked there with my uncle. I worked at herding and whatever interested me. Nothing was forbidden to me. I did read, but stopped when it got heavy. I ran a boat on the sea for three summers. What I needed from songs I did not know. And during that time my health got better. I went to study in Anadyr, entering the technical course on reindeer. I hoped to get back to the tundra. Meanwhile I had one teacher, Valeria Ostapenko, who taught botany during the day and in the evenings gathered people at her home to sing. I attached myself to her, sang a lot, and performed.

"When I got home I couldn't go back to the tundra because my father was ill and I had to look after him. A fellow showed up and I got married. The reindeer stayed in the tundra and I . . . ! I began to work in the club, organizing an ensemble. It was not easy in Enmelen because people there were from all over, gathered at the time of collectivization. In other villages where there is more continuity of tradition the work is easier—the ensembles go of their own accord. But in Enmelen and Nunligran I have to keep after them. Somewhere I found an old book and taught myself to play the *bayan* [a type of accordion]. I met a composer from Magadan who helped me. I had a big question. You see, I listened to a lot of music—I love the classics, Beethoven, Bach, Tchaikovsky. Something wasn't working out. They asked me to come and study in Moscow, but by then I had children and couldn't go. And then I started working with these old songs and things started to work out. Composers helped me to ensure that I wasn't letting these other influences spoil my folk music. Now I don't play as much, but before music was everything."

Next day I ran into Alexandra Sokolovskaya. "Why she has to behave like that I just don't understand. Such an artiste! Who does she think she is?" I promised her a copy of my tape, because one of the annoying factors in our recording session had been that Sokolovskaya's machine was working poorly, making a lot of noise.

Then I went on to see Tagrina. "What is the matter with that woman?" she complained. "She calls herself cultured, and then all that smoke, and all that noise. What a shame. We had an opportunity to do so much . . . !" So we sat down and drank more tea. I learned more about the ins and outs of how the school system had worked to teach everybody Russian and to weaken the Chukchi language. The Chukchi textbook that came out was based on a dialect different from their own. And with the exception of the Chukchi language class, everything else was taught in Russian, which at first the children did not understand at all. Their first teacher was a Chukchi, but nobody liked him much.

The second teacher was a remarkable Russian named Nosov. He learned the Chukchi language and even ate the local food. Well, what could he do, exclaimed Tagrina—there was no cafeteria and he had no wife! This schooling was for the first four years, before Tagrina went to Providenia to the boarding school where she got so sick.

Nosov took part in the sports competitions. Tagrina's father took young men under his wing for about four years and trained them thoroughly. He also watched their diet. Drinking tea would make you weak, he said. After the war things got bad in the village; alcohol came in and people stopped training.

Nosov was a great friend of Tagrina's brother, she recounted. The brother was cheerful and smart, and he sang and danced. In those days the men used to go up the hill from the village and watch for walrus. When they saw one they would rush down and go out in their boats to catch it. The first one to see the walrus called out, and everybody came running. When the weather was good they wouldn't even get specially dressed for the sea. One day the brother went out—he was a good shot with a rifle, and strong and good with the harpoon. But that day, out in the boat, someone shot him from behind. The one who shot him was that first teacher, the Chukchi nobody liked. There was some sort of jealousy between them, perhaps because the brother also appealed to women.

The shot went into his lung, and he lost much of the use of his left arm and several fingers. This did not prevent him from playing the *bayan*, but he never fully recovered. This was one of the factors that led their father to give up on life. He was already discouraged by the decline in the young men he used to train. And then there was the unexpected death of his wife, Tagrina's mother.

"Mother used to walk from this place where we were living, twelve kilometers to Enmelen for groceries. It took about two hours each way.

"At the place where she fell there is a road now, but then there was just a path. It was a place where a lot of snow gathered." She left on April 26 to get supplies for the May 1 holiday; the family had decided to celebrate at home instead of going to Enmelen. Some time after she left, people heard a loud noise like an avalanche. Everyone knew you should shoot to bring an avalanche down before you passed a dangerous place, but apparently she didn't, and it landed on her. Tagrina came home from school and found out that her mother had gone. At the other end the family learned that she had arrived in town and left on the twenty-eighth. They searched. Maybe she had gone to visit people in the reindeer brigade. But no. Tagrina herself searched, and at one point fell into snow up to her hips. She fell over backward and saw the sea far below her. A young man pulled her out. They searched for nine days and didn't find the mother. The only thing that was ever found was her walking stick, washed up by the sea. They could tell it was hers because one of the children had scratched her name on it.

After telling this sad story, Tagrina left the next morning at seven to catch the helicopter. Her daughter and I imagined her that very evening eating walrus meat at home.

Soon after that, I departed myself—back to the land of Pacific salmon and espresso coffee. I was relieved to see the lights of Nome, after that deceptively short flight from Providenia that took me to a different world. Relieved and at the same time saddened.

Reflecting on the differences in life in these two neighboring parts of the north, I began to debrief myself. The culture shock I experienced on my return to the overwhelming commercialism of North America was greater than the shock of seeing conditions in Chukotka when I had arrived there. I noticed our wastefulness and the fact that people on the other side are technologically behind us and at the same time ahead in some human skills and moral perception. And then began the process of translating not only the stories but the world in which they were told.

Chukotka's rich storytelling tradition is amazingly resilient. A hundred years ago tales and legends were told at holiday celebrations, during special evenings set aside at trade fairs, and in *yaranga*s and subterranean houses filled with children and adults. Men told stories while hunting, as they waited for good weather or for animals to come; they called animals to them with their stories. Women told stories in the home while waiting for winter to end; they used stories to teach children and to exchange knowledge about the art of living. The spiritual gift of storytelling was revered along with the shamanic gift—storytellers had the power to call spirits, to raise courage, and to heal physical and spiritual ills.

Stories contained the history and worldview of the Chukchi and Yupik peoples. They taught the origins of life and the relationships among the many beings and forces that live on the earth. This teaching has a different quality from that of the classroom—learning comes from the inside. Those who grow up in an oral tradition say that the stories have helped them to think for themselves rather than to rely on outside authority.

It would be a serious mistake to look at the picture of life as it was a hundred years ago, which the stories convey, as monolithic tradition, unchanged through hundreds or thousands of years. Even before the arrival of Russians and other outsiders, the cultures of Arctic Asia had been shifting and adapting, like cultures everywhere. Contacts with other indigenous peoples, movements across continents, environmental conditions, trade, wars —all had their effect. But the changes of the twentieth century have been faster and more radical than those that went before. Traditional holidays, regular trade fairs, the nomadic lifestyle, the traditional family structure— all are gone. *Yaranga*s and subterranean houses hardly exist. They have been replaced by schools, museums, "houses of culture," and apartment buildings. An atheistic, "scientific" worldview prevails in cities and towns under the influence of a dominant culture from the outside.

The occasions for storytelling are different now—but what about the purpose? Much of today's storytelling is going on in schools and in other situations involving children. Viktor Tymnev'ye, Alla Panaug'ye, Valentina Rintuv'ye, Svetlana Chuklinova, Nina Trapeznikova, and Nina Notai are just a few of the many people actively involved in transmitting traditional values and information to a younger generation. The teaching function of stories remains strong, even if the setting has become more pedagogical and purely practical. In fact the teaching function has taken predominance over others that were more important in the past. Dance ensembles are another place where this transmission of values and information happens—theatrical versions of old tales are created in which children themselves participate.

Elders such as Naukeke, Kutylina, and Nununa are consulted regularly. Although some of them complain that nobody listens to them but ethnographers, increasingly their own young people are turning to them, recognizing the importance of their knowledge—both historical and spiritual. Because so many elders have already died, the ethnographic work of the past is consulted as well. Many elders still practice ancient skills: healing with herbs and chants, finding out who has been reincarnated in a newborn child. They are carrying on the historic and spiritual function of the story-teller. Chuklinova's divination through dreams shows that the younger generation is carrying on some of these traditions. My own experience in other parts of Siberia since 1994 shows that the historical function of storytelling has become more important as people recover a positive self-image.

Vital to the process of preservation and renewal of culture is the middle generation—people like Takakava, Tagrina, Ainana, and Nakazik, who remember the old ways at least in part and at the same time have completed a higher education and are integrated into the modern world. Writer-storytellers such as Itevtegina and Kymytval bring themes from old tales into contemporary literature, developing its artistic side and bringing the past into the present.

The themes reflected in today's storytelling reveal much about contemporary concerns. Which stories do people tell during times of economic and social breakdown? Which values do storytellers feel are needed to guide their people through this difficult transition? The courage not to give up is crucial to survival. Good hunting techniques, wisdom and loyalty, finding the other side in what appears evil, and good relationships with animals are valued. There are many reminders in today's tales that the despised orphan comes out on top, and about what goes into finding a good marriage partner. One of the things that helps people survive is the ability to look at trouble with a sense of humor.

One traditional tale conspicuous in its absence is that of the girl who refuses to marry. Although there are many tellings of this story in collections, I heard only one version, and that from a man. Nakazik's version did not include the usual conclusion in which the girl is resurrected or creates a new clan, but instead ended in tragedy. Today's storytelling world seems to have little room for a woman's directing her creativity outside marriage and child-rearing, although women are at the heart of the cultural revival. Women tellers seem to prefer to enourage men by telling their heroic tales, and I heard four versions of the most common theme in male stories—that of the despised orphan. The people of Chukotka are spending the winter in the bear's den.

An interesting process emerges in which life stories become legends, following old patterns. We saw this in the way Tagrina described her ancestor as a despised orphan, and in the way Itevtegina described her father's heroic deeds. Panana's independence in hunting and running the supply boat as she grew up in Sireniki follows the theme of independent women of the past, and she is admired by younger people for it. It could be that when cultures with sacred stories are suppressed, they find new ways of carrying on their philosophy—or it could be that legend-making has always worked this way. Through story, the experience of sacred times resonates in life. Tales of the time of creation are transformed into creative life stories in present time.

The many anecdotes told about shamans are a major source for legends about crossing boundaries between the spiritual and the everyday. Although shamans were not much in evidence in Chukotka in 1993–94, their ability to heal and to help hunters was actively remembered by Kutylina, Takakava, Panaug'ye, Sokolovskaya, Notai, Tagrina, and others. Tales not only about shamans themselves but about the beliefs that inform the shaman's world— such as the transmigration of souls and the importance of dreams—were told and retold.

A middle stage in the process of legend-making, somewhere between myth and everyday life, is represented by Chuklinova's story of the man who wintered in the bear's den and Nakazik's tale of the two brothers. Both possess a quality of having happened to real people, and yet they are just beyond the range of the teller's memory or personal knowledge. Although highly unusual in the course of daily events, the things described are in no way supernatural and could have happened. As Nakazik himself said, "When much time goes by, events from life turn into real tales."

Reflecting again even later, I see how the stories I heard spoke to my personal condition in Chukotka. I know from experience that tellers always aim the story specifically to the listener, and there is no reason to think I was any exception. The stories I heard taught me how to hunt correctly, how to be patient, and how to accept aid from unexpected sources. They even gave me the sense of wintering in the graveyard.

Notes

INTRODUCTION

1. The *v* sound in these words is actually somewhere between the English *v* and *w* sounds. It is a bilabial *v* pronounced between the two lips, not between lower lip and upper teeth as in English or Russian.

2. I have chosen to use the names for these peoples that are most familiar to English-speaking readers. The word *Chukchi* comes from their own name for the reindeer breeders: *chauchu,* "rich in reindeer." They call the shore-dwelling Chukchi *añgalit,* "sea people." The Yupik are called Eskimosy in Russian and variants of Yupigyt and Yuit among themselves.

3. The color red was particularly important for traditional clothing because it is the color of life-blood.

4. Slezkine 1994:105.

5. Forsyth 1993:197.

6. Kendall, Mathé, and Miller 1997:14.

7. Krupnik 1996:35–36.

8. Slezkine 1994:162.

9. Slezkine 1994:159.

10. Vakhtin 1994:40–41.

11. Slezkine 1994:250.

12. Forsyth 1993:200.

13. Slezkine 1994:131.

14. Nikolai Vakhtin, personal communication.

15. Slezkine 1994:174.

16. Slezkine 1994:173.
17. Vakhtin 1994:51.
18. See chapter 2.
19. Vakhtin 1994:55.
20. Slezkine 1994:239.
21. Vakhtin 1994:46.
22. Vakhtin 1994:60.
23. Vakhtin 1994:60.
24. Vakhtin 1994:51.
25. Krupnik 1987.
26. Igor Krupnik, personal communication, 1997.

1 / ANADYR

1. This is the story of the man who married a polar bear, recounted by Bogoras (1975b:112).

2. Many ethnographers say the Chukchi did not have clans. Although they did not have clan names or a requirement to marry outside one's own clan, they did live together in groups of related families. To a degree this is still so, as I saw in Tavaivaam and on visiting the reindeer herders.

3. Since the fall of the Soviet Union, many foreign religious groups have been doing missionary work in Russia. Although some are beneficial, others have been accused of deceit and unethical practices—extorting money and offering courses in things such as business management that turn out to be Bible study.

4. Among the Chukchi, Raven most often functions as a culture hero and trickster, rather than as creator. See chapter 5.

5. For a story in which Fox tricks Bear, see Lena Naukeke's "Raven and Mice" in chapter 3.

6. See Lyuba Kutylina's stories of entering another world by looking into a crack in the earth, chapter 5.

7. Other differences between male and female tellers include the fact that men tell more historical legends than women do. See Viktor Tymnev'ye, chapter 3.

8. A second version of this story appears in Margarita Takakava's collection (1974). It is translated in this volume under the title "Kurkyl and Nuteneyut" in chapter 2. In that version neither Raven nor Fox has a family, and there is a difference in the moral, which emphasizes obedience. A third section shows more about relations

with spirit, and with people, too. Yet another version of this tale appears in Bogoras's collection (1975b:193), where Raven and Fox are married to each other. In this version, Raven flatters the sea spirit while Fox laughs at him.

9. In one creation tale recorded by Bogoras (1975b:153), Raven creates land and sea animals from wood chips after creating the earth by defecating.

10. Some of Rytkheu's stories have been translated into English (Rytkheu 1977).

11. One of these Northwest Coast stories is that of Dzungwa, similar to the tale of "Six Girls and the Giant" told by Svetlana Chuklinova in chapter 4.

2 / KANCHALAN

1. Raven is called Kuikiniaku in the Koriak language and Kurkyl in Chukchi. In both languages his wife is Miti.

2. Turkic and Mongolian yurts share this spiritual orientation, with the entrance facing the sunrise. The parts of the Even shaman's *choom* correspond not only to the cardinal directions but also to the upper and lower worlds and the parts of the body. Each of these structures has a male and a female side.

3. The Chukchi had names for twenty-two cardinal directions, corresponding to the times of day, which begin with Morning Dawn. Only noon and midnight are unchanging; the others move with the seasons. The most prominent benevolent spirits are those who receive sacrifices in these twenty-two directions (Bogoras 1975a:172, 303).

4. Ainana, personal communication, 1994.

5. Bogoras 1975a:174.

6. See "The Girl Who Married a Whale," chapter 7.

7. For example, the tale that appears as the epigraph to this book.

8. Others reside in hair, breath, and the name. Buriat shamans say one type of soul corresponds to the aura.

9. See "The Two Brothers," chapter 6.

10. The spider appears as a helper in three tales collected by Bogoras (1975b:49, 91, 118). He cites the spider as the creator of women, whereas Raven created men (1975b:153).

11. The story reminds me of an Inuit story in which a girl who refuses to marry gets her flesh eaten away while she is underwater. She becomes a skeleton who is revived by a shaman. In the Bogoras Eskimo collection (1975c:419), a man brings a woman to life under the sea. This is related to the circumpolar myths of the sea goddess Sedna.

12. A similar tale was told to me in 1994 by Gleb Nakazik (see "Reindeer, Crow, and Evil Spirit," chapter 6). A much longer version appears in Bogoras's work (1975b:155; the first part also in 1975c:431), in which the hare retrieves the sun, which has been stolen by a *kelye*. The evil spirit chases the hare, who is rescued by an eagle. Instead of turning into a hitching post, the *kelye* is pounded into the ground by the hare.

13. Goodchild 1991:12. Similarities and differences between raven stories in Asia and North America are discussed in chapter 5.

14. Cruikshank 1990:2–44; Goodchild 1991:12–14, 38–43, 110–15.

15. Russian *polog*.

16. The connection between the three worlds is usually made through the polestar.

17. Bogoras (1975a:430–31) described three types of shamans, called *engenggetlen* in Chukchi: those who communicate audibly with spirits (healers and mediums), those who "look into" (clairvoyants), and those who produce incantations. The last were frequently women. Many seasonal holidays, rituals, and healings were performed without the aid of a professional shaman. Every household had a drum, and most people could drum and sing to heal themselves and others. Chukchi shamans are also reputed to have changed sex, usually from male to female (Bogoras 1975a:450–51). This change not only gave a shaman a psychological wholeness but also set him or her irrevocably apart from society.

18. Bogoras 1975a:546. The *č* is pronounced *ch,* and the *š* is pronounced sh. According to Bogoras, the *ś* is a palatalized sound pronounced like *sy.*

19. A *kerker* is a one-piece outer garment worn by women.

20. Told in 1963 in the village of Neshkan by the storyteller Keglilgyny. Transcribed by Y. Atchitagin and translated from Chukchi into Russian by M. K. Takakava (1974).

21. This story was told by an unnamed teller to Lyubov Uvarovskaya and was originally published in Uvarovskaya 1992:23–25.

3 / TAVAIVAAM

1. The idea of the lower world's being sinful must be a late addition, influenced by Christianity. Nowhere else in Chukchi beliefs does it occur. Usually the lower world is either another version of our own, inhabited by spirits, or the land of the dead, which is not thought to be sinful.

2. Before the Soviet period, each Chukchi person had one name. These names have been preserved sometimes as first names and sometimes as surnames. In the

case of the older generation it is usual to call a person by that one Chukchi name, whereas younger people use name, patronymic, and surname in Russian fashion.

3. See chapter 7.

4. See Itevtegina, chapter 1; Tagrina, chapter 8.

5. This tradition is also well known in Central Asia, where the shoulder blade of a sheep is used. A bone from an animal that belonged to the questioner contains the best information about that person's affairs.

6. Meat was stored over the winter in holes in the ice.

7. See "The Orphan with Sharp Hands" (chapter 5), "Two Brothers" (chapter 6), and Tagrina's story of Tuptek (chapter 8).

8. That image appears in Bogoras 1975b:79. See also the epigraph to chapter 2.

9. Chaussonnet 1988:212.

10. Bogoras 1975b:75–77.

11. Goodchild 1991:21, 92; Bogoras 1975b:76.

12. Allen 1989:5–6.

4 / PROVIDENIA

1. The cleansing properties of sacred fire, related to the life-giving sun, are known in many parts of Siberia and North America.

2. The image of a finger drawing a line that turns into a river appears in Bogoras 1975b:40.

3. This image appears in a different story in the Bogoras collection (1975b:107).

5 / CHAPLINO I

1. The Yupik language does not have gendered pronouns. This sometimes causes confusion in translation. At this point Lyuba was referring to the baby as "she" in Russian, whereas it later became clear that the baby was a boy.

2. Normally a *yaranga* does not have a corridor like those in the subterranean houses. Either she is using the word *yaranga* to describe the older kind of Yupik house or she uses to word *corridor* to refer to the cold part of the *yaranga*.

3. A version of this story appears in the collection made by Bogoras almost a hundred years ago (1975c:426). It was told by Nipe'wgi at the village of Unisak on Indian Point. In the Yupik language Chaplino was called Unisak. In that version, the first man the mother meets hits the baby with his big penis, which he also uses to

chop down the tree. The teller explains that the boy could not fly like an eagle at first because he put the eagle suit on incorrectly. There is no grandmother in that version, and the girl argues before giving up her baby.

4. This story is similar to one in the Bogoras Chukchi collection (1975b:98).

5. Meletinskii 1981.

6. "Raven and Mice," chapter 2.

7. Chowning 1962.

8. *Kamlanie* is Russian and comes from the Turkic word *kam,* shaman. In the Amur River region I have seen shamans ask other people take up the drum and dance before the ceremony begins, specifically to make the shaman laugh. This helps raise the energy necessary to call spirits.

9. There are some interesting differences between this version and the one Menovshchikov recorded from the thirteen-year-old schoolboy Tagikaka in 1940. In his version, it is the eagle's idea to bring the young ravens to him, not their mother's. The eagle then explains *why* they should not fly to the north, telling about the gray eagle. When they go to the brother for help, first the adventure of getting there is described—looking down at the ocean as if from an airplane. Then the brother subjects the boys to rigorous physical training before they are ready to approach danger. All of these things are more likely to be on the mind of a young boy than of a grandmother.

10. For more on clothing, see chapter 3. In some Siberian tales, animals are portrayed as people who wear animal skins when they come near humans.

11. Menovshchikov's collection contains the story of a flying shaman, told by Ykaluk in 1971 at Nunyamo village. Ykaluk was sixty-five and spoke the Naukan dialect. Interestingly, the shaman's name was Kutylan, and he lived in Chaplino. While going to a neighboring settlement for food when supplies were low, he met and competed with a shaman named Asisak who had flown from Tygygak in Alaska. The two men exchanged amulet bags in proof of their meeting, and after that Kutylan gained greater shamanic power—now he, too, could fly and do many other amazing things that had not been in his power before his meeting with the flying shaman. The same story appears in the Bogoras collection (1975b:17), but the shamans have different names.

12. The girl was probably not completely undressed but was wearing a traditional *kerker* with the sleeve off from one shoulder. The container for "hiding" meat is the kind used for putting meat away for the winter.

13. See Naukeke, Nakazik, and Tagrina in this volume, among others.

6 / CHAPLINO II

1. Bogoras 1975a:41.

2. *Obshchezhitie* literally means common living place.

3. Some versions of "The Girl Who Married a Whale" (chapter 7) begin with the girl's refusal to marry.

4. Menovshchikov 1974:209.

5. Menovshchikov 1974:31.

6. The black sorcerer is distinguished from a "black shaman," a concept better known among the Turkic and Mongolian peoples. Although shamans, like sorcerers, can do harm, it is generally considered to be against their code of ethics, and they are more often remembered as doing good.

7. "Raven, Kelye, and Hare," chapter 2.

8. The Bogoras Chukchi collection (1975b:85) also includes a tale in which a young man changes sleeping places with a girl and then cuts off the head of the girl's mother.

7 / SIRENIKI

1. Krupnik 1991:3–4.

2. Bogoras 1975a:254–56.

3. Some scholars see connections between the designs in the tattoos and the petroglyphs of the lower Amur River and of Tuva. A. N. Lipskii looks for an ancient cultural center in Southeast Asia from which the images spread northward to the Bering Strait and into North America, and northwest to the Yenisei River (Devlet 1976:19).

4. Menovshchikov 1985:238–41.

5. The Chukchi writer Yuri Rytkheu (1977) tells a version of "The Woman and the Whale" in which she gives birth to both whales and humans. Thus the men who kill the whale kill their own brother. The more usual version has the baby whale killed by people from another clan. It is not clear whether Rytkheu's is a legend or his retelling. Today's hunting taboos come from international law and environmental activists. I have heard people speak disparagingly of "the greens" as people who want to prevent them from doing what they need to do to survive.

6. This passage is from Rasmussen's *Intellectual Culture of the Iglulik Eskimos* (1976:55–56), as quoted by Joan Halifax (1982).

7. Baleen, also called whalebone, is the elastic, horny material making up the food-catching filter in the mouths of baleen whales. In the nineteenth century it was used for corset stays.

Glossary

This list contains words from Chukchi (C), Yupik (Y), and Russian (R).

achak (Y). Oil lamp.
ayut'ka (Y). Cutting board.
baidara (Y). Traditional boat covered with walrus skin.
bayan (R). A type of accordion.
chottagin (C). Outer part of a *yaranga*.
enmen (C). Word spoken at the beginning of a Chukchi tale.
etset' (C). Word spoken at the end of a Chukchi tale (women's pronunciation).
kamlanie (R, from Turkic). Shaman's ceremonial activity.
kelye (*kelkh*) (C). Evil spirit.
kerker (C). Chukchi women's outer clothing, made of one piece.
Kilvei (C). Chukchi spring holiday.
kolkhoz (R). Cooperative collective farm.
obshchezhitie (R). Communal dwelling.
olak (Y). Woman's knife.
shaman (R, from Tungus). Traditional healer, diviner, and ceremonialist.
sovkhoz (R). Wage-based collective.
stroganina (R). Shaved frozen fish.
teviskhin (C). Beater for getting snow out of fur clothes, made from reindeer antler.
tungak (Y). Evil spirit.
vezdekhod (R). All-terrain vehicle.
yaranga (C). Traditional Chukchi dwelling.
yoroñi (C). Internal sleeping compartment of a *yaranga*.

References Cited

Aarne, Antti, and Stith Thompson
1973   *The Types of the Folktale.* Folklore Fellows Communications no. 184. Helsinki: Soumalainen Tiedeakatemia.

Allen, Paula Gunn
1989   *Spider Woman's Granddaughters.* New York: Fawcett-Columbine.

Bogoras, Waldemar
1975a   *The Chukchi.* Jesup North Pacific Expedition, vol. 7. Memoirs of the American Museum of Natural History. New York: AMS Press.

1975b   *Chukchi Mythology.* Jesup North Pacific Expedition, vol. 7. Memoirs of the American Museum of Natural History. New York: AMS Press.

1975c   *The Eskimo of Siberia.* Jesup North Pacific Expedition, vol. 8, pt. 3. Memoirs of the American Museum of Natural History. New York: AMS Press.

Chaussonnet, Valerie
1988   "Needles and Animals: Women's Magic." In *Crossroads of Continents,* edited by William W. Fitzhugh and Aron Crowell, pp. 209–26. Washington, D.C.: Smithsonian Institution Press.

Chowning, Ann
1962   "Raven Myths in Northwestern North America and Northeasten Asia." *Arctic Anthropology* 1(1):1–5.

Cruikshank, Julie, in collaboration with Angela Sidney, Kitty Smith, and Annie Ned
1990   *Life Lived Like a Story: Life Stories of Three Yukon Elders.* University of Nebraska Press; Vancouver: University of British Columbia Press.

Devlet, M. A.
1976   *Petroglyfy Ulug-khema* (Petroglyphs of the Ulug-khem). Moscow: Nauka.

Forsyth, James
1993   "The Peoples of Siberia." In *The Forgotten Peoples of Siberia,* edited by Gunther Doeker-Mach, pp. 193–202. Zurich: Scalo.

Goodchild, Peter
1991   *Raven Tales.* Chicago: Chicago Review Press.
Halifax, Joan
1982   *Shaman: The Wounded Healer.* London: Thames and Hudson.
Kendall, Laurel, Barbara Mathé, and Thomas Ross Miller
1997   *Drawing Shadows to Stone.* New York: American Museum of Natural History.
Krupnik, Igor
1987   "Bowhead vs. Gray Whale in Chukotka Aboriginal Whaling." *Arctic* 40(1).
1991   "Extinction of the Sirenikski Eskimo Language." *Inuit Studies* 15(2):3–22.
1996   "The 'Bogoras Enigma': Bounds of Cultures and Formats of Anthropologists." In *Grasping the Changing World: Anthropological Concepts in the Postmodern Era,* edited by Václav Hubinger, pp. 35–52. London: Routledge.
MacDonald, Margaret Read
1982   *The Storyteller's Sourcebook: A Subject, Title, and Motif Index to Folklore Collections for Children.* Detroit: Neal-Schuman Publishers and Gale Research.
Meletinskii, E. M.
1981   "Paleoaziatskii epos o Vorone i problema otnoshenii Severo-Vostochnoi Azii i Severo-Zapadnoi Ameriki v oblasti fol'lora" (Paleoasiatic epic about Raven and the problem of the relationship between northeast Asia and northwest America in the realm of folklore). In *Traditsionnye kul'tury Severnoi Sibiri i Severnoi Ameriki* (Traditional cultures of northern Siberia and northern America), edited by L. V. Kiseleva, pp. 182–200. Moscow: Nauka.
Menovshchikov, E. M., ed.
1974   *Skazki i mifi narodov Chukotki i Kamchatki* (Tales and myths of the peoples of Chukotka and Kamchatka). Moscow: Nauka.
1985   *Skazki i mifi eskimosov* (Tales and myths of the Eskimos). Moscow: Glavnaya Redaktsiya Vostochnoi Literatury.
Rytkheu, Yuri
1977   *Reborn to a Full Life.* Moscow: Novosti Press Agency Publishing House.
Slezkine, Yuri
1994   *Arctic Mirrors: Russia and the Small Peoples of the North.* Ithaca: Cornell University Press.
Takakava, Margarita K., ed.
1974   *Kto samii silnii na zemlye?* (Who is the strongest on the earth?) Magadan: Magadanskoe Knizhnoe Izdatelstvo.
Thompson, Stith
1955–58 *Motif-Index of Folk Literature: A Classification of Narrative Elements in Folktales, Ballads, Myths, Fables, Mediaeval Romances, Exempla, Fabliaux, Jest-Books, and Local Legends.* Rev. ed., 6 vols. Bloomington: Indiana University Press.

Uvarovskaya, Lyubov P.

1992 *Skazanie Sela Snezhnoe* (Tales from Snezhnoe village). Edited by N. Vorontsova. Anadyr: Regional Center for Folk Culture.

Vakhtin, Nikolai

1994 "Native Peoples of the Russian Far North." In *Polar Peoples: Self Determination and Development*, pp. 29–80. London: Minority Rights Publications.

Suggestions For
Further Reading

Allen, Paula Gunn

1986   *The Sacred Hoop.* Boston: Beacon Press.

Baboshina, O. E.

1958   *Skazki Chukotki* (Tales of Chukotka). Moscow: Gosudarstvennoe Izdatel'stvo Khudozhestvennoi Literatury.

Dikov, N. N.

1974   *Ocherki istorii Chukotki s drevneishikh vremen do nashikh drei* (Essays on the history of Chukotka from the most ancient times to our day.) Novosibirsk: Nauka.

Fienup-Riordan, Ann

1994   *Boundaries and Passages: Rule and Ritual in Yup'ik Eskimo Oral Tradition.* Norman: University of Oklahoma Press.

Fitzhugh, William W., and V. Chaussonnet

1994   *Anthropology of the North Pacific Rim.* Washington, D.C.: Smithsonian Institution Press.

Fitzhugh, William W., and Aron Crowell, eds.

1988   *Crossroads of Continents.* Washington, D.C.: Smithsonian Institution Press.

Forsyth, James

1992   *A History of the Peoples of Siberia.* Cambridge: Cambridge University Press.

Grant, Bruce

1995   *In the Soviet House of Culture.* Princeton, N.J.: Princeton University Press.

Krupnik, Igor

1993   *Arctic Adaptations: Native Whalers and Reindeer Herders of Northern Eurasia.* Hanover, N.H.: University Press of New England.

Levin, M. G., and L. P. Potapov, eds.

1964   *The Peoples of Siberia.* Chicago: University of Chicago Press.

Oakes, J., and R. Riewe

1998   *Spirit of Siberia: Traditional Native Life, Clothing and Footwear.* Vancouver: Douglas and McIntyre.

Pika, Alexander

1989   "The Small Peoples of the North: From Primitive Communism to 'Real Socialism.'" In *Anxious North: Indigenous Peoples in Soviet and Post-Soviet Russia,* edited by Alexander Pika, Jens Dahl, and Inge Larsen, pp. 15–33. Copenhagen: IWGIA.

Reid, Bill, and Robert Bringhurst

1996   *Raven Steals the Light.* Seattle and Vancouver: University of Washington Press and Douglas and MacIntyre.

Slezkine, Yuri, and G. Diment

1993   *Between Heaven and Hell.* New York: St. Martin's Press.

Wood, Alan, and R. A. French

1989   *Development of Siberia.* New York: St. Martin's Press.

Index of Motif Types

This index, compiled by Michael Ballantyne and Murray Shoolbraid, is offered to enable readers to compare the motifs found in the tales in this book with motifs found in world folktales already catalogued by folklorists. The motifs listed appear in the tales and legends I collected, in beliefs and anecdotes related in conversation, and in stories I have summarized from published sources. Although many folklore motifs appear worldwide, they often have different meanings in different cultures. Drawing analogies between indigenous cultures and those such as the European that have come under the influence of dualistic world ideologies, including Christianity, can be particularly risky.

The motif index numbers are based on Stith Thompson's *Motif-Index of Folk Literature* (1955–58). Because Thompson's work did not include tales from the area covered by this book, some motifs appear that have not been catalogued previously. Index numbers followed by a plus sign (+) refer to new motifs with a suggested general position in Thompson's index; numbers followed by an asterisk (*) are suggested additions with a specific position in the index. Motifs in brackets [...] do not appear in this book but are are included in order to justify the position of a proposed new motif. The page numbers in the right-hand column refer to the pages of this book.

The stories in this book also represent three of the tale types identified by Antti Aarne and Stith Thompson in their *Types of the Folktale* (1973). The story "The Evil Yaranga" in chapter 6 compares well with their type 327B, "The Dwarf and the Giant," and also with their type 1119, "Ogre Kills His Own Children." The story "Raven and Fox" in chapter 1 compares well with Aarne and Thompson's type 1960E, "The Great Farmhouse."

177

E. The Dead

F. Marvels

Motifs Unrelated to Established Index Numbers

Index

Page numbers in boldface indicate illustrations.